FOLK FESTIVALS AND THE FOREIGN COMMUNITY

Print by Svanström, Stockholm

FOLK FESTIVALS AND THE FOREIGN COMMUNITY

by

Dorothy Gladys Spicer

Department for Work with Foreign-Born Women,
National Board, Young Womens Christian Associations

The Womans Press
600 Lexington Avenue
New York, N. Y.

Republished by Gale Research Company, Book Tower, Detroit, 1976

COPYRIGHT 1923 BY
THE NATIONAL BOARD OF THE YOUNG WOMENS
CHRISTIAN ASSOCIATIONS

**Library of Congress
Cataloging in Publication Data**

Spicer, Dorothy Gladys.
    Folk festivals and the foreign community.

    Reprint of the 1923 ed. published by the Womans Press
New York.
    Bibliography: p.
    1. Festivals. 2. Festivals--United States.
3. United States--Foreign population. I. Title.
GT3930.S6   1976   394.2'6973   70-167201
ISBN 0-8103-4301-0

IN GRATEFUL APPRECIATION
OF THE GENEROSITY
OF
MY FRIENDS FROM OTHER LANDS

INTRODUCTION

The ear of a race is strangely attuned to some particular note. Every drop of blood runs to it and every nerve dances with it. The squealing of the bagpipe arouses atavistic memories and brings back heath and heather—thatch and scone. The Gypsies' fiddle lures the last penny out of the Magyar's pocket and brings to his drab mill town in Pennsylvania memories of the Czardas and the Puszta. A minor note like a gentle sigh restores to the Slovak the lost gladness of home. A tremulous, high tenor note visions the sky of Italy to the millions who shall never see it again. A deep wailing cadence like that which comes from the surge of suffering gives the Jew that sense of joy which is akin to pain. All these notes must be woven into the gladness of the new Race which is being born here in America out of many race strains and divergent cultures.

These race strains and divergent cultures find their finest expressions in the various festivals which in the Old World bring colorful joy into the hard, everyday life of toiling folk. The aesthetic sense is a great and unsatisfied hunger in the hearts of most of our immigrant peoples; to help them to satisfy it, to rescue it when the clatter and crash around them begin to make them cal-

INTRODUCTION

lous, is a great and useful and patriotic task. It means the preservation of our great cultural resources.

For this reason I welcome Miss Spicer's book and commend it to all those who are trying to find a key to the heart of the foreigner and who wish to help make accord in our discordant racial conglomerate. The author has been wise in the selection of her material, clear and concise in the directions she gives for production, and inspiring in the good and gracious spirit which permeates the book.

The American genius for organization is needed to restore and preserve the great cultural values which have been brought here, and to make possible the living together of these people who once were aliens and enemies and have to be made into citizens and friends.

EDWARD A. STEINER.

TABLE OF CONTENTS

I. THE FESTIVAL AND THE RACE 1
   An Old Tradition in a New World.
   Universality of the Folk Festival.

II. WHAT IS THE FOLK FESTIVAL? 9
   General Character.
   The Festival versus the Pageant.

III. THE SOCIAL SIGNIFICANCE OF THE FOLK FESTIVAL 14
   A Means of Aesthetic Approach to the Foreign-Born.
   An Interpretation of Foreign Parents to their Children.
   Festal Remnants in America.
   Community Value of the Festival.

IV. FOLK FESTIVALS IN THE MAKING . . . 25
   Choice of Subject.
   Gathering the Material.
   Conserving the Results.

V. THE TECHNIQUE OF FOLK FESTIVAL PRODUCTION 35
   Stage Setting and Place of Production.
   Committee Organization.
      General Director—Committees on Publicity—Business Arrangements—Stage Management—Costuming—Music and Dances—Make-Up.
   The Community Workshop.
   Rehearsals.
   Programs and Tickets.

TABLE OF CONTENTS

      Performance Organization.
      Behind the Scenes—In the Wings—With the Orchestra—On the Floor—General Hints for the Director.

VI. FESTIVAL EXPERIMENTS IN FOREIGN COMMUNITIES. 65
      The McKeesport Folk Festival of Early Spring. Festivals Tried and Proven.

VII. THE TRIUMPH OF SPRING—A FESTIVAL OF OLD WORLD SONGS AND CEREMONIAL RITES 79
      Appendix.

VIII. THE EVE OF ST. JOHN—A MIDSUMMER FESTIVAL OF DANCE AND SONG 97
      Appendix.

IX. THE FEAST OF INGATHERING—THE HARVEST HOMING OF MANY PEOPLES . . 117
      Appendix.

X. FOLLOWING THE STAR—A FESTIVAL OF YULETIDE SONGS AND CUSTOMS IN MANY LANDS 129
      Appendix.

SELECTED BIBLIOGRAPHY OF FESTIVAL MATERIAL 147

CHAPTER I

THE FOLK FESTIVAL AND THE RACE

An Old Tradition in a New World

America has an opportunity no other country has ever had,—the opportunity of assimilating the old traditions of many lands into a new tradition of her own. In the complexity of our modern industrial life we have well-nigh lost the seasonal consciousness which has so potently influenced the development of other races. Our great cities are so congested and the pressure and tension of the daily routine is so tremendous that little heed is paid to the significance of the passing seasons. All months are the same!

The festival was the channel through which early man poured forth his wonder at the ever changing months, his fear lest darkness fail to give place to light and his gratitude for final deliverance from the terrifying forces of nature which surrounded him. Through the medium of the folk festival, therefore, we in America may preserve much of the mysticism, idealism and beauty of other peoples.

THE FESTIVAL AND THE RACE

Universality of the Folk Festival

From country to country the festal theme has been variously interpreted according to the distinctive characteristics of the land. Everywhere, however, its same essential aspect has been retained. The solstices, the equinoxes, planting of seed and ingathering of crops have become festive occasions observed through ritualistic dance, procession and song.

Winter, the harbinger of plague, disease and misfortune, unconsciously became associated with death. Hence the widespread custom of beating, burning or carrying out in effigy figures representing winter, death, carnival, Lent, Judas, the Easter Man and others gradually developed from the ancient cult of the vegetation spirit. It has become almost universally customary to destroy the effigy of death amid curses, jeers and threats and to usher the spirit of spring into the villages with triumphal processions, songs and dramatic contests between summer and winter. Rejoicing takes the place of mourning and the revival of vegetation is heralded with merrymaking and laughter.

> "For lo, the winter is past;
> The rain is over and gone;
> The flowers appear on the earth,
> The time of the singing of birds is come,
> And the voice of the turtle-dove is heard
>   in our land."

THE FESTIVAL AND THE RACE

The summer solstice is celebrated throughout Europe on June twenty-fourth, by the Feast of St. John. As the sun reaches its highest point in the sky at this season, primitive man associated the fire symbol with the festival. On the Eve of St. John, consequently, huge bonfires are kindled in almost every land. In some countries, torchlight processions wend their way around the fields to stimulate the growth of crops and to keep evil forces at a distance. In Norway, peasants light their bonfires in the belief that thus they can banish disease from the cattle; in France, young people leap through the flames so the flax or grain may grow as high as they are able to jump; in Ireland, peasants throw a lighted sod into the fields, to protect the crops from blight. St. John's Eve is essentially a festival for driving away evil spirits, for protecting crops and animals and for insuring a plenteous harvest.

Since Biblical times, when the Lord gave the commandment to "keep . . . the Feast of Ingathering which is in the end of the year when thou hast gathered in thy labors out of the field," autumn has been regarded as a period of peculiar rejoicing over the safely gathered grains.

The Feast of Ingathering is still observed in orthodox Jewish communities of this country. Booths or tabernacles, covered with green branches, are erected in some of our largest cities

THE FESTIVAL AND THE RACE

to commemorate the forty years' sojourn in the wilderness when tents provided the only shelter for the Children of Israel. Palm branches and citrons are taken to the synagogues as an offering to the great Giver of fertility whose command to keep the harvest feast has been heeded throughout the ages.

The end of the harvest is indeed a festival of thanksgiving in every country. In Czecho-Slovakia, *posviceni*, or harvest celebrations, are observed in different villages from the middle of August on into the autumn. A church service of thanksgiving is held, and every household, according to its means, prepares special cakes, a roast pig, a goose or other holiday dishes. The festivities end with dancing and singing at the village inn. Czecho-Slovaks in America regard our Thanksgiving as *posviceni* and every girl in service feels she must spend that day under her parents' roof.

Armenians in this country continue to observe the time-honored custom of blessing the new grapes on the Day of the Holy Virgin which falls on *Navasart*, the ancient Armenian New Year. A service of thanksgiving for the grape harvest is held in the churches. Prosperity for the coming year is invoked. The grapes are blessed and later distributed among the sick.

The festival of the winter solstice, like that of

THE FESTIVAL AND THE RACE

midsummer, is universally symbolized by fire. The sun has well-nigh run his course through the heavens; the days are short and gloomy and the powers of darkness are striving to gain supremacy over the forces of light. In every country man has reasoned that the sun might best be aided in the last weary days of his struggle by merrymaking, feasting and the burning of many lights,—for the deepest gloom of midwinter holds a promise of renewal of life and length of days. In this belief have the lighted candles of Christmas-tide, the illumined tree and the blazing Yule log had their origin.

In our own country many remnants of ancient Yuletide festivals may yet be found. Syrians in our American cities observe, on December fourth, the symbolic feast of lighted candles for Saint Barbara. "Every year we hold the Feast here in this room," the father of eight children told me. "St. Barbara was a good girl; her faith and love toward God make her an example to the children." A table is arranged with sweetmeats prepared from nuts, sugar, honey and wheat—the last in memory of the dead and significant of the resurrection of the soul. Small lighted candles give the Feast a gay appearance. The doors are opened and girls, boys and grown-ups, led by a white-clad figure representing St. Barbara, enter the room, chanting as they march around:

Holy St. Barbara,
Thou chosen of God,
Thy stern heathen father, adorer of stone,
Determined to kill thee;
But God was thy Shield.
Thy father's keen sword,
When he sought to behead thee,
Was changed to a necklace of coins most rare;
The rope used to hang thee
Became a silk girdle,
And the fire to burn thee,
As sweet incense ascended.
Holy Saint Barbara,
Thou chosen of God.[1]

Chanukah, or the Jewish Feast of Lights, marks the beginning of the eight-day festival in honor of the recapture of Jerusalem and the temple by the Maccabees. Prayers are said in the synagogues at sunrise and sunset. In the homes a taper is lighted each night until, by the eighth night, eight candles are burning in token of ever increasing strength.

The Carpatho-Rus (Rusin) choir boys of one of the churches in McKeesport, Pennsylvania, go from house to house at Yuletide bearing an illumined "Bethlehem," or manger scene, and singing songs of good cheer. A somewhat similar custom is observed in Biddeford, Maine, by Greek school boys on January first, the Day of Saint

[1] English version by the author.

Basil. They carry a gaily decorated toy boat, "St. Basil's ship," symbolizing the vessel in which the good saint made his voyage from Caesarea. The boys collect pennies in the boat as they chant greetings such as the following:

> St. Basil comes and passes by,
> And scorns us for no reason why;
> He comes from Caesarea town;
> Mistress, bring us something down.
>
> . . . . .
>
> The New Year follows on Christ's birth;
> So holy Christ, who walks the earth,
> May bless you, every girl and boy,
> And fill all good hearts with joy.[1]

Many of our American homes place burning candles in the windows on Christmas Eve in remembrance of the old Christian legend that the Christ Child passes by and must be lighted on his way lest He stumble in the darkness. This custom, like the burning Yule log and the illumined tree, is but a modern reminiscence of the ancient fire festival of the winter solstice.

Thus it may be seen that the festivals of original significance to the race have gradually expanded and developed according to the varying customs and traditions of different lands. The

[1] Folk Songs of Many Peoples, by F. H. Botsford. The Womans Press, New York, 1922. Vol. II, p. 326.

THE FESTIVAL AND THE RACE

fundamental character of the seasonal festival remains the same, however, whether it is celebrated in the Old World or in the New. Rejoicing in the renewal of life in early spring, hope in the future harvest, thanksgiving for the garnered grain and feasting and merriment because days of light are near at hand—these are festal tendencies common to the heart of every race.

CHAPTER II

WHAT IS THE FOLK FESTIVAL?

GENERAL CHARACTER

The drama, art and music of the peasant folk embody those fundamental impulses, conflicts and emotions of human nature which are the basic elements of all great artistic production. The folk festival is the simplest and the most democratic of all forms of dramatic expression. It presents the unification of pantomime, dance and song, of color, rhythm and sound, through a common theme of deep emotional or religious significance. The folk festival includes all phases of peasant art. It affords the greatest flexibility in subject and variety in interpretation to the foreign community worker seeking to preserve the picturesque customs, folklore and music of other lands. It gives an opportunity for the self-expression of the group rather than of the individual and of the entire community rather than of the chosen few of marked dramatic ability.

THE FESTIVAL VERSUS THE PAGEANT

A confusion exists in the minds of many people regarding the distinction between the festival and the pageant. The festival is the direct, straightforward and naïve dramatic expression of the peasant folk; the text may not be found in books, since the festival is the outgrowth of existing folk life in a given group or community; it is the emotional outpouring of spontaneous action and is deeply expressive of the joy and sadness in the hearts of the participants.

The pleasure of a festival is by no means confined to those taking part but reflects unconsciously upon the audience. Festivals were never *made;* like Topsy they *just growed.* I once witnessed a spring festival in a prosperous Pennsylvania town, where the director rather nervously confided to me before the performance that "she didn't quite know how things were coming out because the foreign people had planned everything by themselves." The success of the evening proved to her that she could trust the foreign groups to work up their own festivals. Little more than the original theme was followed. Each nationality expressed itself after its own fashion. Numberless unforeseen episodes and songs were introduced to suit the mood of the participants. The Slovak gypsy musicians, in American costume, who were engaged to play accompaniments for the dances and songs of their people, became so filled with enthusiasm that they insisted upon standing on the stage with the rest of the per-

WHAT IS THE FOLK FESTIVAL?

formers. These wild-eyed, brown-skinned wanderers from across the sea played with a fire and passion which made the audience unconsciously sway to and fro to the rhythm of the music. One of the gypsy fiddlers so forgot himself that he almost danced with the costumed groups for whom he was playing. The musicians became an integral part of the festival and were instinctively included by the performers in all the folk customs which followed. The Italian group, not to be outdone by the Slovaks, entered into their parts with so much naturalness and abandon that one felt as if one were once again witnessing a festival under Italian skies. Now and then the Italian members of the audience would break into song as they listened to their native melodies. Each nationality in succession interpreted the return of spring and the renewal of life in a spirit of joyousness and good fellowship. The festival expanded in the process of presentation and the enjoyment of the actors was mirrored in every careworn face in the audience. On that night Slovaks, Italians, Germans, Greeks, Poles and Americans were united by a bond of common brotherhood through the delineation of Old World folk rites and ceremonial customs.

The pageant, unlike the festival, is primarily a splendid spectacle; it consists of the formal presentation of an historical event or group of events or the symbolic representation of an idea, virtue or principle of life. The pageant is undemocratic, since it is generally the creative production of a single mind instead of the artistic expression of an entire group or community: the actors in a pageant, moreover, because of the conventionalized form of the production, generally lack the unconsciousness and naturalness which is perhaps the greatest charm of those taking part in a festival.

The confusion existing in people's minds between the festival and the pageant may well be illustrated by an experiment made some time ago by two foreign community workers in a town where two-thirds of the population were foreign. It was decided to try a folk festival as the possible means of bringing together, for the first time, the foreign- and American-born of the city in a community interest.

The workers sketched out a plan for a Christmas festival in which the modern Yuletide customs of the nationalities represented in the city were united by the spirit of that first Christmas of long ago. The festival as a whole was put under American leadership, while the community workers directed the parts of the foreign groups. The final result was an interesting study in two conflicting points of view, although the affair did not fail in its primary objective of welding together foreigners and Americans in a community enter-

WHAT IS THE FOLK FESTIVAL?

prise. The old-fashioned, formal, pageant tendencies kept cropping up throughout the festival. The wish for spectacular effect was more predominant than was the desire for a simple, straightforward presentation of the folk idea. How much more effective the festival might have been had coarse straw rather than decorative palms indicated the crude birthplace of the Christ Child; had a chorus behind the scenes sung the heavenly message instead of human angels with flowing hair and tinseled wings; and had the "Spirit of Christmas" been felt by the audience through the unity of the festal theme rather than seen in the flesh! The folk festival seeks to suggest rather than to imitate and to symbolize rather than to reproduce. It stimulates the imagination of the audience by the very simplicity of its form and thus excludes the striving for show and effect which is the keynote of pageant production.

CHAPTER III

THE SOCIAL SIGNIFICANCE OF THE FOLK FESTIVAL

A Means of Aesthetic Approach to the Foreign-Born

There is no more certain method of approach to the heart of the foreigner with whom the community worker comes in touch than through the best the foreigner has to give,—through his festivals and songs, his art and handicraft, his folklore and traditions. A bond of fellowship and understanding will be created whenever we make a sincere effort to share these fruits of the spirit and wherever there is a consistent striving on our part to enter into that ideal life which, after all, is his real life. It is impossible for us as Americans to find a point of contact with the foreigner in our community until we have achieved in some measure, at least, an appreciation of his festal background, so full of vivid imagination, so rich in emotional value and so deeply tinged with the idealism of other lands.

A keen appreciation and a sympathetic knowledge of folk festivals of other countries is of vital importance to the foreign community worker.

SOCIAL SIGNIFICANCE

Such appreciation and knowledge are bound to quicken the imagination, to create mutual understanding and to foster a deeper comprehension and love of the foreigner. When someone spoke to an old German gardener about his love for flowers he replied, running his fingers through the petals of a huge prize chrysanthemum, "Oh! I love him not, he not grow." This is indeed true of our relation with the foreigner,—if we love him not, he not grow. Let us seek to love him through a more intelligent understanding of those festal days which are his heritage from an earlier civilization.

An Interpretation of Foreign Parents to Their Children

The cultural and spiritual background of the foreign father and mother is thoroughly interwoven with their Old World home customs, holidays, festivals and saints' days. Oftentimes in this country we are able to observe festivals, originating in other lands but transplanted to new soil, which show to a rare degree the idealism and sentiment of the foreigner. Through a careful study of the rich festal heritage of the older generation, the foreign community worker may help solve the baffling problem of how to get acquainted with the parents of those boys and girls of American birth who have scornfully cast

SOCIAL SIGNIFICANCE

aside the colorful language and symbolic customs of their forefathers and have all too rapidly assimilated the movie, jazz and gutter speech of the modern American city.

Foreign mothers are often very young and very lonesome. Because of their close confinement to the home they assimilate American ways and language slowly and are soon looked down upon by their children, who grow intolerant of the "old-fashioned" ways of their mothers. One of the best methods of bridging the ever widening gulf between foreign parents and children is to seek out and preserve the festival customs of the different nationalities in a given neighborhood. Such a procedure will teach the younger people a new reverence and respect for the race, language and traditional background of their parents and will make them more sincere in the appreciation of their distinctive racial heritage of music, dance and song.

A group of young Italian girls was once asked to take part in a spring festival in a certain dreary industrial town. Their interest was half-hearted; none of them knew how to dance the *Tarantella;* rehearsals dragged and failure seemed imminent. Finally it was suggested that the girls practice at home with their parents, who would doubtless remember all the difficult steps. Not only did the girls learn to enjoy the dance which they finally

SOCIAL SIGNIFICANCE

presented with unusual grace and charm, but they were taught a keener appreciation of the artistic contribution of the Italian race to American culture. When the festival was past, one girl confided to the director, "I used to hate everything Italian but now I love it."

Festal Remnants in America

An interest on the community worker's part in the festivals of the foreign mother will make her feel that she is being of definite service to the neighborhood and love is always fostered through service. Moreover, the recollection of the beloved customs of the homelands is a source of real pleasure to the strangers within our gates. As a Lithuanian mother once said to me after telling me in broken English how she celebrated many of her feast days at home, "Thank you for coming. Come again. My husband and I will dance for you and I will tell you the whole history of Lithuania."

Every community where peoples from other lands are gathered together, whether in country, town or large industrial city, contains a priceless store of festal material. The neighborhood furnishes the subject matter for the festival program. The foreign community worker has but to delve deeply into the hidden folk life of her people and she will discover undreamed-of riches. The

SOCIAL SIGNIFICANCE

Greeks of Tarpon Springs, Florida, for example, each year celebrate the Feast of the Epiphany in Old World, ceremonial fashion. A procession, led by the priest bearing the golden cross, goes to the river bank where an arch of green foliage has been erected. After the benediction the cross is thrown into the waters, whence it is recovered by young men of the town. Bulgarians of Steelton, Pennsylvania, perform a similar ceremony on the banks of the Susquehanna River.

Serbians in this country regularly do honor to St. Sava on the twenty-seventh of every January. Special services are held in the churches in memory of the educator saint, congratulations are exchanged, friends are visited and songs are sung in commemoration of St. Sava.

Each year, on July sixteenth, Italians of the United States observe the Feast of the Madonna del Carmine. The upper Italian quarter of New York City is gaily lighted by festoons of green, white and red electric lights. Push carts, loaded with strings of Spanish chestnuts, piles of pink and white cakes, *torrone* and watermelons, line the streets, which are thronged with worshippers, fortune-tellers and sightseers. Brightly decorated wax replicas of different parts of the human body are sold from booths near the Church of the Madonna del Carmine, where they are presented as votive offerings.

SOCIAL SIGNIFICANCE

The examples given illustrate only a few of the many feast days still observed by foreign peoples in this country. They will suffice, however, to suggest some of the manifold resources from which the foreign community worker may draw original material for local folk festivals.

Community Value of the Festival

The community value of the presentation of folk festivals based on Old World customs, beliefs and traditions, naturally falls under four distinct headings,—spiritual, artistic, social and educational.

According to a legend[1] said to be taken from a sixteenth century Russian chronicle, when Christ, the Guardian of Beauty, was about to ascend to Heaven, some troubadours approached him and asked, "Lord Christ, to whom art Thou leaving us? How can we exist without Thee?" Christ answered, "My children, I shall give thee golden mountains and silver rivers and precious gardens and thou shalt be nourished and happy." But then St. John approached Christ and said, "O Lord, give them not mountains of gold and rivers of silver. They know not how to watch over these treasures and someone rich and powerful will steal them away. Instead, leave thy children but thy name and thy beautiful songs and com-

[1] From English version by Nicholas Roerich.

mand that all who value thy songs and love thy singers shall find the open gates to Paradise." And Christ replied, "Yes, I shall give them not golden mountains but my songs, and whoever appreciates them shall find the open gates to Paradise."

The folk festival furnishes a spiritual outlet for the pent-up creative ability of the foreigner who is so crushed under our modern industrial system that he has no opportunity for spontaneous self-expression. Through presenting the well-loved songs, dances and customs of the homelands, dulled eyes brighten, tense muscles relax and the weary worker in factory or mill "shall find the open gates to Paradise." By means of the festival the foreigner is given a chance to express his artistic cravings and to free his spirit of the constant repression inflicted upon him by the exigencies of daily breadwinning. The spiritual value, then, of the folk festival and its reaction on the foreigner cannot be overemphasized.

A festival admits of just as much artistic variety as there are personalities among the performers. Almost every known art and craft may be employed in the costuming, stage setting and lighting of a festival as well as in the working out of dances, songs and pantomimes. A community workshop where people of many different nationalities come together day after day for the

SOCIAL SIGNIFICANCE

sake of designing and making stage properties and costumes is a source of never-ending inspiration. Often the work may have to be explained through an interpreter or through that universal language of signs and smiles, since many of the foreign people speak little English. Unity of purpose and originality of production will always be characteristic of the workshop, however, and the hours spent there will be filled with comradeship and good cheer.

It has many times been demonstrated that the folk festival is one of the best means of discovering hidden artistic talent among foreign people. For example, a Croatian barber in a large Pennsylvania mill town was found to be a composer as well as the conductor of a Croatian Tambourica Orchestra. He gladly wrote special music for a certain spring festival, orchestrated several folk songs and left his business in order to conduct rehearsals. His orchestra was drawn from Croatians working in the mills. An Albanian baker in a small New England town became so inspired with the idea of a festival in which the songs and customs of his people were to play an important part that he took charge of the entire Albanian episode and spared no time nor pains in rehearsing the children in their songs. A group of Hungarian girls, determined to produce a scene characteristic of their country, worked

SOCIAL SIGNIFICANCE

out their own national costumes with unusual accuracy and artistic skill.

The fact that the festival is a practical means of doing away with individualism and of developing the talent of all rather than of the few is perhaps one of the strongest arguments in favor of its social value. The festival, moreover, fosters a spirit of coöperation which brings individuals, races and institutions together in a common community interest. Peoples habitually nourishing a deep-rooted race hatred toward one another forget their prejudices, jealousies and petty strifes in the effort to accomplish an end in common. A rather remarkable festival was given in a small Maine mill town where French Canadians and Russian Jews, Albanians and Greeks, Americans and Italians harmoniously united in the presentation of the Yuletide theme. The Jewish boys and girls dramatized the Old World *kolyada* custom at the beginning of the New Year and were radiantly happy to have an equal share in a festival of many peoples. Both the parents and the local Rabbi gave full permission to have the children participate and for one night, at least, the ever present barrier between Jew and Gentile was effectually eliminated.

The educational value of the festival is of equal importance to the community worker and to the foreign groups. A festival teaches the community

SOCIAL SIGNIFICANCE

worker that only the most careful research methods are applicable to the gathering together of the folk customs and traditions of her neighborhood. She learns that a Slovak girl will not appear in a Czech national costume even though she comes from the Republic of Czecho-Slovakia; that the Maypole of a Piedmontese village lad has a more intimate significance to him than the village Maypole of the Scandinavian peoples; and that the Slovaks and Slovenes, though Slavs, do not necessarily belong to the same nation though the names are somewhat similar! The community worker is taught through the festival a deeper understanding of race psychology than she before possessed and, best of all, she is taught to look below the surface into the very hearts of foreign people. The dull exterior of a weary-eyed Italian may hide the soul of a musician and the little, white-faced French milliner of the neighborhood store may be a creative genius.

Through the medium of the folk festival the foreigner is taught the value of organized recreation. He is at last convinced that there is a new and better way to play than to spend his time and money in the stifling dance hall, the movie theatre or on the street corners of the crowded cities. The foreigner realizes that the America of his neighborhood appreciates something of the beauty and culture of the Old World. A new and whole-

SOCIAL SIGNIFICANCE

some outlet for his excess energy is provided and joyousness and freedom of spirit take the place of sordidness and greed. The festival, moreover, not only teaches the younger generation of American birth a love and respect for the customs and traditions of the parents, but develops an appreciation and knowledge of the essential qualities in the art, music and poetry of peoples from other lands.

CHAPTER IV

FOLK FESTIVALS IN THE MAKING

CHOICE OF SUBJECT

The folk festival is not a cut and dried, "ready-to-wear" art product. For this reason it is almost impossible to find on the shelves of the local public library a festival adaptable to the individual needs of the foreign groups in a particular locality or town. The community worker is therefore confronted with the unique problem of directing the talent and ability of her people toward the upbuilding of an original festival based on the traditions, customs and beliefs of her own neighborhood.

If a festival is planned to include a number of different nationalities, it is always advisable to choose as the central theme a seasonal motive of international significance. Having selected such a subject, it is easy to introduce the songs, dances and rites of different countries in order to illustrate how a certain festal occasion is observed in various parts of the world. The festival thread should hold the racial episodes together in an easy, logical fashion. Simplicity and straightforwardness must always be sought and all complicated allegorical allusions must be avoided. Once the central theme is determined, encourage the foreign groups to use the utmost individuality in the interpretation of their own parts. Always keep in mind, however, the dramatic unity of the production as a whole. Illustrations of seasonal festivals will be found in the four suggested outlines given in succeeding chapters.

In case a single nationality is to present a festival, a rare wealth of material will be found in native folk and fairy tales cloaking the nature theme, in ancient nature myths and in legends woven about a seasonal motive. For example, a German group might symbolically work out a spring festival based on the tales of Snow White or the Sleeping Beauty. The object is not realistically to reproduce the story, but rather to present through pantomime, dance and music a poetic interpretation of the folk tale in its relation to the seasonal motive. The group should itself evolve the dramatic form of the festival, and dances, songs and costumes should be characteristic of the nationality taking part.

A Greek group might appropriately choose the myth of Demeter and Persephone as the basis of an autumn festival. The legend of the fern, blossoming but once a year on the Eve of Ivana Kupala, would make a dramatic nucleus about which a charming Russian midsummer festival might be woven. Various versions of the almost international myth of St. George and the Dragon, symbolizing the conflict of summer and winter, might be interestingly interpreted by different races. Whatever the subject chosen for the folk festival, the nature element should always be emphasized. The subject, moreover, must harmonize with the season in which the festival is given. Speaking detracts from the impersonal charm of the production. Foreign people who have been in this country only a short time, if obliged to speak in an unfamiliar tongue, lose the natural poise and freedom of movement invariably characterizing their pantomime. Always remember that simplicity is the keynote of folk festival success and that a simple idea, well produced, is of far greater aesthetic value to performers and audience than a complicated subject, bunglingly presented and fundamentally lacking in unity of conception.

GATHERING THE MATERIAL

A festival should be planned some months in advance in order to make possible a careful survey of foreign community resources. It must be remembered from the very outset that it is a means to an end and not an end in itself. It is the method of making possible a more intimate knowledge of foreign people, of bringing together races of diverse customs and beliefs in a united community interest and of approaching that great store of Old World culture and beauty which remains closed to all but those endowed with sympathy and understanding.

A preliminary survey of the foreign community may be started through consulting local telephone books, directories and the files of various organizations interested in work among the foreign-born. In this way the names and addresses of prominent foreign business and professional men, churches, theatres, lodges and folk dance or singing societies may be obtained. After the first few personal contacts are made, the survey work will progress almost automatically, as each foreigner you visit will refer you to others possessing further facts. The more varied the sources of information obtained the more satisfactory the result will be. Consult the Czecho-Slovak college professor on the Easter customs of his village as he remembers them from boyhood days, but do not forget to ask your scrubwoman how the Easter cakes were made, or fail to inquire about the Easter pussywillows from the humble Bohemian florist around the corner.

When seeking to find out about a certain folk custom with which you yourself are unfamiliar, avoid too many questions, in order that the simple-minded peasant woman may be saved from the embarrassment of feeling that you are hopelessly ignorant and heartlessly curious about her country and ways. If she is tactfully led on, the points about which you desire information will be gradually drawn out. It is always better to listen to what the foreigner has to say than to talk too much yourself. Always approach the person you are interviewing in the deferential attitude of one wishing to learn and to share. Never carry the impression that you wish to "Americanize"! Seek especially to know the older men and women, who are found to possess a more accurate knowledge of folk dances, customs and legends than the younger generation which has grown ashamed of the colorful racial background of its forebears.

In visiting the homes of the peasant folk, make a practice of dressing simply and of adopting a gentle, sympathetic attitude. Accommodate yourself to the home customs of different nationalities and show yourself scrupulously particular in the observance of all forms of foreign etiquette, no matter how unnecessary they may seem to you. Do not evince surprise if you are kissed on both cheeks by a Mohammedan woman the first time you enter her household, and do not fail to sit down and break bread with an Oriental family before taking your departure. Customs which may seem trivial to you possess a deep significance to the foreign woman, with whose religious belief and physical welfare they are oftentimes indissolubly linked.

Never appear hurried, even though you find yourself turning mental somersaults in order to catch the next suburban train. The foreigner cannot be rushed or forced and the more quickly you cultivate a calm, placid exterior the sooner you will find it possible to collect the desired data. Take time to inquire about the welfare of the members of the household and to exchange the formal salutations peculiar to a certain race. You will find that the foreign person never forgets to be courteous. When visiting in his home, why should you not show him the courtesy and consideration which are expected of you?

When seeking information about a certain custom or belief, never seem incredulous at the replies you receive. Remember that you are a student of foreign psychology, that you are learning directly from people instead of books and that your opportunity for obtaining facts will be proportionate to your receptiveness of spirit and openness of mind. If a Syrian woman tells you that her lump of dough turns to leaven on the blessed Epiphany Eve or a Bulgarian mother insists that telling the baby it has a pretty face will cause the evil eye to be cast upon it, do not laugh but sympathetically nod your head and murmur, "Ah, to be sure." It is more than likely that by

FESTIVALS IN THE MAKING

this means you will learn many facts which will aid you in comprehending the superstitious foreign practices and unaccountable prejudices which are well-nigh inexplicable to the American mind.

Wherever visits are made in quest of festival data, tactful inquiries should be made regarding original peasant costumes, shawls or aprons brought to America from other lands. Such precious articles as these are not often visible to the curious eye of the casual caller. Perhaps they are tucked away in some dusty trunk or heavy chest whence they are exhibited on very special occasions. The community worker who wins the confidence of the foreign people in their homes will discover many hidden treasures in the way of colorful caps, gay skirts and dainty bodices which will add the crowning touch of genuineness to the proposed festival.

The best method of obtaining accurate knowledge of folk festivals is to attend as many foreign weddings, plays, church ceremonies and holiday festivities as your community affords. You are not likely to find notices of these events in American newspapers, but your foreign friends will invite you to their entertainments and holiday celebrations when they know you are sincerely interested and are assured you will attend in sympathetic spirit. No spectacle, for example, could be more impressive or suggestive for processional possibilities on the stage than the Holy Saturday candlelight ceremony observed each year in New York City at the Greek Orthodox Church; no folk dances could be performed with more grace and abandon than those the foreign students introduce into their festivals at American colleges and no scene in folk life could be more touching than the funeral processions which wind slowly through the Italian quarter of lower New York City.

Another excellent method of getting a vivid impression of the folk festival atmosphere is by inviting groups of women of different nationalities to meet together at your International Institute, Neighborhood House, Settlement or Social Centre, as the case may be, in order to talk over their holidays and holy days, to sing their folk songs and to dance their native dances. Through first inspiring your audience with a mental picture of the festival plan, all shyness is soon forgotten; every woman is eager to tell you about the customs of her own country and women of one nationality become as interested in hearing about the customs of other lands as in relating their own; a lively competition of folk songs arises, and foreign mothers, whose feet have long been unaccustomed to dance the beloved rounds of the home village, soon forget their lack of practice in their eagerness to demonstrate a certain half-forgotten step.

FESTIVALS IN THE MAKING

As a result of these informal international gatherings, the community worker endowed with imagination and sympathy of spirit will see her folk festival unfold before her very eyes.

CONSERVING THE RESULTS

Unless your festival fails of its ultimate purpose it will serve as a real internationalizing influence in the community. It will mean much to you and to your foreign friends. See that the contacts made through the festival are not dropped but are adequately followed up and maintained.

Your festival will probably lead to an intimate acquaintance with national groups previously untouched by your work and will give you the opportunity of forming new clubs, classes and study groups. The awakened interest in folk customs, dances and songs may be advantageously employed as a nucleus for recreational and educational programs. Story telling classes, based on the fireside folk legends of the foreign grandfather and grandmother, will prove stimulating for the younger girl who has drifted away from the old people in her home. Folk dance and song groups will be a source of new enjoyment to the foreign woman who has languished in the New World where nobody seems to care for her except in relation to the number of buttons she can sew on in an hour or the amount of piece work she can accomplish in a day.

One of the invariably important results of a festival is that it links together, for the first time, in many instances, the American- and foreign-born of the community in an enterprise of mutual interest and enjoyment. It stimulates in the American a revitalized appreciation of the poetic imagery and imaginative beauty of the foreigner's cultural background. It is for the community worker to see that this appreciation is nurtured and kept alive through giving the American people additional opportunities for meeting their Old World neighbors at play.

Ultimately a festival may even result in the opening of a neighborhood playhouse in the very heart of the foreign district, where peoples from many lands gather to create beauty; where a community workshop is the common meeting place of craftsman, artist and peasant in the skillful production of those gentle Old World arts which are little known in our country; and where the music, drama and dance of other races may be cherished and preserved for future generations. Your festival may mean this and more besides, for beauty of the spirit is without end.

CHAPTER V

THE TECHNIQUE OF FOLK FESTIVAL PRODUCTION

STAGE SETTING AND PLACE OF PRODUCTION

The matters of determining the character of the stage setting and the place of production come next in consideration after the choice of theme and the gathering of the festival material. If the festival is to be given in spring or summer, try to have it out of doors in a local park or open space where natural scenery provides a picturesque and suitable background. In communities affording no park, a section of the athletic field or tennis court may be converted into a fitting stage through employing a moveable stage set. A set which has proved adaptable to many seasonal festivals is semicircular in form and measures forty feet across. A wooden lattice twelve feet high, with doors two and one-half by nine feet inserted at regular intervals, forms the background. The doors are made by stretching muslin or canvas over wooden frames hinged to the background and are painted in bright Slavic colors in keeping

TECHNIQUE OF PRODUCTION

with the character of the individual festival. Fragrant branches are woven through the latticework and hung over the doors. Brilliant natural or artificial flowering vines and blossoms are carelessly fastened among the green. The general effect produced is that of a row of charming village cottages. The suggested set is appropriate as described for spring or summer festivals. For harvest time the lattice background is covered with red and yellow autumn leaves and for winter with branches of pine or evergreen interspersed with artificial poinsettias. In case it is impossible to have a forty-foot stage, the width of the set may be reduced and one of the doors may be omitted. Chicken wire may be substituted for the lattice background if desired. The same set is adaptable for use either out of doors or indoors.

When the festival is to be given indoors, select as large a platform or stage as is available, since folk dances and customs may be more effectively reproduced when given plenty of room. If, on the other hand, the stage is small and there is no space and perhaps no money to construct the suggested set, plan just as simple and unobtrusive a background as possible. Place in a semicircle wooden poles in firm standards at regular intervals on the stage floor. Stretch heavy wire from pole to pole at the top and fasten securely. From this wire suspend by curtain pins hangings of soft

TECHNIQUE OF PRODUCTION

old blue, dull gray-green or brown flecked with gold. The latter combination gives the effect of broken color, which is more successful in the absorption of light than a plain color. The curtains may be made from dyed canton flannel, burlap or painted unbleached muslin and should be abundant enough to hang in soft folds.

Always avoid cluttering properties or gaudily painted scene sets. Have everything that is essential, but nothing more. The use of a drop curtain between episodes is heartily discouraged, since additional simplicity of effect and feeling for the peasant spirit is obtainable through making all scenery shifts before the eyes of the audience. Low, gaily decorated benches may be placed opposite each other at the right and left of the stage in such a way that they will not interfere with the action on the stage. Two or three children in bright peasant costumes occupy the benches during the performance and make all scene shifts between episodes in formal, ceremonial fashion. For instance, suppose a fireplace indicates an indoor scene and the change to out of doors is desired. When the performers have left the stage, the scene shifters advance toward each other, bow, clap their hands, step backward with characteristic folk dance step, and then go about their duties on the stage, singing, meanwhile, the words of some ancient labor folk song.[1] The children bring out and set before the fireplace a wooden screen, painted in simulation of a gray stone wall, thus converting the indoor scene into a suggestive exterior. Once more advancing toward each other, they bow, clap their hands and dance back to their benches, where they sit during the next scene. The necessary scenery shifts are in this manner performed with a quaint precision and a delicate charm which become as much a part of the audience's enjoyment as the festival itself. The shifts, moreover, are regarded by the audience as short intermissions revealing a bit of folk background thoroughly in harmony with the fundamental idea of the festival.

Committee Organization

GENERAL DIRECTOR: The choice of a director is of the utmost importance to the success of the festival, since this person comes into intimate touch with the home life and customs of the various foreign groups taking part. She must therefore be selected with especial care, because of her tact, freedom from racial prejudice and sympathetic approach to peoples differing widely in type and belief. An understanding of foreign psychology is more essential on the part of the festi-

---

[1] See labor songs in Folk Songs of Many Peoples, by F. H. Botsford. 2 Vols. The Womans Press, New York. 1921-22.

TECHNIQUE OF PRODUCTION

val director than a technical knowledge of dramatic production. Technical skill, although unquestionably a great asset, is not absolutely essential for successful results. A person with a sense of humor, who can tactfully settle racial differences, who has the ability to inspire others with the vision in her own mind and who steadily works on toward final accomplishment with calmness and gentleness of spirit will inspire foreign people with confidence and be able to draw from them the hidden talents they may possess.

After the preliminary survey of the community has been made and the various groups have been cultivated in the manner suggested in Chapter IV, the director ought not to find it necessary to allow more than three or four weeks for the period of actual rehearsal. She should, however, plan to organize her committees three months in advance of the time of performance, in order to reap the fullest benefit of the festival as a community enterprise. Three months' preparation is a desirable average period but should by no means be regarded as a hard and fast rule, since the time allotted for preliminary work depends largely upon the type of festival chosen and the ability of the individual workers. It goes without the saying that a festival *well planned* and *planned in time* possesses greater finish and deeper significance to the community than a slap-dash per-

TECHNIQUE OF PRODUCTION

formance regarded as an ultimate end in itself. Remember that it pays to prepare and that careful organization at the outset saves much needless confusion, annoying worry and senseless nerve strain at the last minute.

The festival director should choose the chairmen of her various committees with due regard to their fitness for the work to be accomplished. It is wise to have both an American and a foreign chairman on some committees, since by this means greater unity of thought and action is assured. Have both men and women on your committees and let them include presidents of foreign folk dance and singing societies, milliners, costume designers, newspaper editors, and other prominent business and professional people. The greater the variety of interests you have represented, the more certain will be the success of your festival.

The chairmen of the various committees are responsible to the director, who should furnish each with a typewritten card containing the following information: Name of committee, name of chairmen and those serving on the committee, duties of committee outlined *in full*. By adopting this simple device everyone knows what he or she is expected to do and no excuse is given for shirking. The director should, from the first, establish a harmonious working relation between herself and her committee chairmen, and should empha-

TECHNIQUE OF PRODUCTION

size the fact that the committee is as important to the success of the production as the performers themselves.

COMMITTEE ON PUBLICITY: This committee should, from the start, be alert to its responsibility for adequate advertising of the festival and for seeing that it is well attended. Emphasis should be placed on oral as well as on printed and visual publicity. The greatest oral publicity is obviously achieved through those taking part in the program. Hence it is advisable to choose the performers with regard to variety of class, interest and occupation. Representatives from the committee should make personal announcements at foreign and American clubs, lodges and societies, libraries, schools and colleges. The local pastors should be interested and asked to mention the festival in their churches. It is almost invariably true that foreign clergymen are so sympathetic with the folk festival idea that they render active assistance through speaking of it in the parish, picking out especially talented members of their choir or congregation as participants and helping in the correct costuming of their own groups. It has many times been proven that foreign priests and ministers are our most reliable co-workers and our best festival advisers.

Printed and visual publicity should be carried

TECHNIQUE OF PRODUCTION

on through newspaper articles, special notices, posters and handbills, announcement films, store window exhibits and town criers. This type of publicity should begin *weeks in advance* and must be kept red-hot throughout the actual period of the festival. News items for the daily papers may include write-ups such as the following:

1. The organization giving the festival; something of its history, activities and its relation to the community as a whole; why it regards the folk festival as a means of approach to the foreign-born.
2. The story of how the proposed folk festival is being worked out with the help of the foreign people of the community; what nationalities are taking part and the special contribution of each. These articles may be illustrated with pictures of the various race leaders or groups in national costume *provided no preference is shown one nationality over another.* This is a matter of the utmost importance, since entire festivals have sometimes been threatened with ruin because the Hungarians' picture appeared in print whereas the Roumanians' did not or because the Slovaks had a good write-up and the Hungarians were slighted. It is difficult for the average American to realize that old

TECHNIQUE OF PRODUCTION

racial prejudices are very strong even though transplanted to new soil and that national jealousies, which are the cause of much bloodshed in Europe, lie dangerously near the surface even in America. The question of nationality write-ups must therefore be handled with so much discretion that a feeling of unity and brotherhood will take the place of the bitterness and dissension which are sometimes found to exist between different nationalities.

3. The director and committee; who they are, their training and experience in community work. Many of your committee people are probably men and women prominent in local community enterprises. Interesting items can be written about them.

4. The names of patrons, patronesses and guests of honor; their reason for showing special interest in the festival.

5. Description of the voluntary work of local corporations or organizations in the cause of the festival. For instance, the mills may have donated material and workmen to construct the stage set or have furnished cotton dress goods for the costumes; the Boy Scouts may have gathered branches for the stage background, or the local drygoods store manager may have lent you properties or cur-

TECHNIQUE OF PRODUCTION

tains from his store. Give full credit to all who have assisted.
6. Complete festival program and names of all those taking part. The program write-up should appear the day preceding the performance.
7. After-festival report, written from the point of view of the group and not of the individual. Remember that a festival is the dramatic expression of everybody in the community and not the work of a few stars.

The Publicity Committee should be responsible for the preparation of special announcement lists to include American and foreign leaders among the foreign-born, social workers, newspaper editors, pastors and their wives, professional men of prominence, well known merchants, presidents of societies and foundations and persons of definite educational interests. Formal printed or typewritten announcements should be used, followed by personal letters or calls where greater interest needs to be stimulated.

Posters and handbills should be freely posted and distributed in the local schools, colleges, clubs, halls, foreign lodges and societies, stores and public buildings. Street cars and busses afford an excellent opportunity for exhibiting posters. In some cities it is advisable to have foreign girls

TECHNIQUE OF PRODUCTION

and women in costume interpret the spirit of Old World life and village customs through store window exhibits. Such a publicity measure as this draws crowds of onlookers who will become much interested in the festival idea. Street criers, in European costume, will also attract much attention and create a sympathetic attitude on the part of many an indifferent passer-by. This method of advertising is employed in Stockholm, where a gorgeously arrayed town crier, bearing bugle and banner, rides through the city streets announcing the folk festivals and dances at the Skansen Out-of-Door Museum.

COMMITTEE ON BUSINESS ARRANGEMENTS: The duties of this committee are to take charge of all business matters relating to the festival; to arrange for the hall, park or field where the performance is to be given; to see to the printing of programs and tickets; to solicit program advertisements, if they are desired; to pay all bills; to provide for ushers, ticket sellers, ticket takers, checking of wraps, floor hostesses, distribution of programs and whatever may be necessary for the pleasure and convenience of the audience.

COMMITTEE ON STAGE MANAGEMENT: One of the most important functions of the Committee on Stage Management is to see that the stage setting is properly constructed and set up. The

TECHNIQUE OF PRODUCTION

coöperation of large corporations and business firms should be enlisted. Oftentimes a mill employing large numbers of foreign people will gladly contribute toward the festival for the sake of demonstrating its good will and sympathy in a community enterprise. If it is your intention, therefore, to approach some public-spirited person on the matter, be sure to have definitely in mind all the things you want and then ask for them; make a clear diagram giving the dimensions of the stage and the plan for the setting. Be definite and accurate down to the smallest detail. If the person you are interviewing sees that you thoroughly understand your business you will probably get more than you ask for. Always have with you a duplicate diagram so you can hand it over at once, provided your proposition is accepted. Business men have little time to spare and appreciate concise information.

The committee is responsible for stage lighting, cues for the electrician, and properties. The general director should provide a complete list of all properties for the different episodes or scenes. The properties must be collected and in their proper places for rehearsals and actual performance. The committee has charge of scenery shifts, moreover, and must give full instructions to persons acting as shifters.

It has been found practical, in consideration of

TECHNIQUE OF PRODUCTION

the American part of the audience, to have large, black and white lettered signs, indicating the nationality which is performing, set up in plain sight during a given racial episode. There are always some in the audience who are unable to distinguish one national costume from another, who lose their places on the program or leave their reading glasses at home. For these persons the sign system has proved a great boon. The signs should be handled by the scene shifters, for whom they are arranged in order of appearance on the stage of the different nationalities. The signs may be set in a standard at one side of the stage where they are visible to all but do not obstruct the view.

COMMITTEE ON COSTUMING: It has been found extremely valuable to appoint a foreign chairman for the costuming of each of the national groups taking part. The different chairmen are responsible to the costume director, who buys materials, plans the sewing periods, has the costumes ready at a certain time, stores them and so on. Inaccuracy in the making of Old World peasant costumes is, to the foreigner, a mark of flagrant disrespect and unforgivable carelessness. Before attempting to reproduce a certain costume every authentic source of information should be studied. Go first of all to the older peasant women who, if they do not possess costumes of their own, will be able to tell just how the head scarf should be

TECHNIQUE OF PRODUCTION

knotted, the shawl adjusted and the folds of the skirt arranged. Ask the families you are calling upon to show you pictures of themselves and their friends in national dress. Old files of the *National Geographic Magazine* may be consulted in any public library and will prove most useful in costuming the various groups. Inexpensive colored prints illustrating Old World costumes, folk festivals and customs should be purchased as suggestive material. If local art dealers do not carry such prints, they may be obtained through Rudolf Lesch, 225 Fifth Avenue, or Albert Bonnier, 561 Third Avenue, New York City. The pictures range in price from twenty-five cents up and may be effectively framed and hung on the walls of your centre after being used for costuming purposes.

It is sometimes advisable to make costumes from crêpe paper since the effect produced under artificial light is of greater delicacy and tonal softness than is obtainable from other materials. Free charts and working instructions for costumes or stage properties will gladly be furnished by the Dennison Manufacturing Company, Service Bureau, New York, Boston, Philadelphia or Chicago. Costumes do not have to be made from expensive materials although insistence should always be made upon accuracy of detail. Effective results may be produced from cheap

TECHNIQUE OF PRODUCTION

materials such as flowered cretonne, cheesecloth, paper cambric and cotton velvet. Each costume should be well constructed, since this makes it available for repeated use. "National Costumes of the Slavic Peoples," published by The Womans Press, New York, 1920, gives excellent practical suggestions for making Slavic costumes, and the same general principles set forth in this book will be found applicable to costumes of other nationalities.

COMMITTEE ON MUSIC AND DANCES: This committee should consist of local foreign and American orchestra directors, musicians and dancing instructors. The chairman should be responsible for gaining the interest and coöperation of the various persons on her committee, should give all orchestra and dance cues for rehearsals and final performance and should see that no confusion results from combining a large number of musicians of different nationalities. It is usually the case that each foreign group wishes to have its own national musicians accompany its part in the program and hence the music problem for a festival differs greatly from that of a pageant or play, where one orchestra suffices for all.

Folk dances should be directed by the foreign people themselves. The older men and women are always delighted to render this service in case there are no professional foreign dancing instructors available.

The music for a festival must be as spontaneous an outpouring of the spirit as the action itself; its value can never be reckoned in dollars and cents. In many cases the interest will be so great that musical services will be volunteered free of charge and such freely given service often proves to be one of the features of the festival production.

COMMITTEE ON MAKE-UP: This committee should be large enough to avoid all last-minute hurry, since make-up cannot be recklessly dashed on under pressure of time. The chairman need not necessarily be a professional person but should be someone of keen artistic sense who is used to studying the lines and expressions of people's faces. She must carefully instruct her committee some time in advance of the performance. Every member should be required to give satisfactory make-up demonstrations before dress rehearsals begin. Folk festivals call for few character parts but these few should be well done; otherwise the general make-up is simple. The performers should never be allowed to make up themselves. The illusion of naturalness from the audience seats must be striven for and too abundant use of rouge and powder discouraged. For all practical festival purposes Stein's make-up has proven most

TECHNIQUE OF PRODUCTION

satisfactory. It may be purchased locally through theatrical costumers or drug stores.

THE COMMUNITY WORKSHOP

In the making of every folk festival there must be set aside a place where all may gather to cut and sew, to model and dye, to design and paint in the interest of the coming event. Though the workshop room be nothing but an old basement or unused office, it should be characterized by the spirit of creative effort and friendly good will which ever draws foreign peoples more closely together. The workshop equipment may be simple. If possible, try to provide a sewing machine with sewing materials, cutting tables, a costume wardrobe, a sink with running water, an ironing board, an electric iron for pressing costumes, a gas plate for dyeing materials, and cupboards for nails, hammers and tools. The workshop should be open during certain hours of every day and evening. Local milliners, costume designers, art and manual training teachers may be pressed into service to take charge of the workshop activities at stated hours during the day or week.

The workshop is the place for cutting patterns, designing and making costumes, fashioning hats, dyeing curtains and constructing properties or scenery. All finished costumes should be labeled with the names of the persons for whom they are

TECHNIQUE OF PRODUCTION

designed and hung on hangers in the wardrobe. On the door a typewritten inventory of the contents should be pasted. Each costume with all its accessories must be separately listed. If the costumes are well made and historically correct, there is no reason why they cannot be rented to other foreign community centres for a nominal fee. The rental proceeds will more than cover the actual cost and will help toward purchasing materials for additional costumes. Every costume sent out should be packed carefully in a box labeled with a slip containing the following information:

1. Nationality of costume.
2. Lent by ....
3. Date ....
4. Inventory of articles contained in box together with a fair value for each article. The value should be estimated not only according to actual cost of materials but also with due regard to the time and labor spent in making them.
5. Statement that the person renting the costume will be held responsible for estimated value of any article lost or damaged.
6. Amount of rental fee. The fee will differ according to the cost and character of the individual costume.

Authentic national peasant costumes are difficult to procure even through professional costumers. Your foreign girls will be interested in

TECHNIQUE OF PRODUCTION

adding to your stock of costumes through the rental method long after the festival is past. Thus the costuming problem of the second or third festival will be much less difficult and expensive than that of the first. In some cases you may find that certain groups wish themselves to buy fine materials and spend many hours in embroidering or braiding them according to the traditions of the home countries. This plan has been found to work out satisfactorily and is highly recommended, since the costumes thus produced are better in quality and more beautiful in workmanship than those ordinarily made. When the festival budget is limited, moreover, it is of great advantage to have certain groups responsible for their own costuming. It also sometimes happens that the foreign people wish to buy outright the costumes they have made in the workshop.

Even the children should be made welcome in the workshop. Little fingers can be trained to fashion many a gay crêpe paper flower or piece of fruit and the delight of the children is great when they see in the final production some small article they have made.

Make the hours spent in the workshop happy hours. Talk freely about the festival plans. Inspire enthusiasm by letting the children "dress up" in their costumes so they can see how they are going to look. Let the whole atmosphere of the

TECHNIQUE OF PRODUCTION

shop be one of cheerfulness, business and comradeship. End the day with a few folk songs, an Old World legend, or coffee and cakes made by the women themselves. Decorate the walls with gay costume prints and have plants growing near the window ledges. Never forget that the peasant heart is starving for beauty,—for color, rhythm and harmony. Beauty is so cheap and all-pervading in European villages; in American cities it is within the means of only the rich. The poorest Scandinavian laborer fills his humble cottage windows with a gorgeous array of potted flowers. The containers may be common tin cans or earthenware pots but the passer-by always lingers and looks back in order to carry away in his heart some of the glory of the peasant window. You can make the good cheer and brightness of the community workshop a high light in the lives of the neighborhood folk who dwell in the darkness and squalor of modern city tenements.

Rehearsals

The skill and ingenuity of the general director are tested to the utmost by rehearsals. Before beginning to rehearse any group, she should tell the story of the festival and make it seem so vivid and worth while that all will be eager to begin work. The director must insist upon strict attention and good discipline. She will have no diffi-

TECHNIQUE OF PRODUCTION

culty in this matter, however, once she gains the interest of her people. She must watch carefully to see that her groups do not become overwearied. Rehearsal periods should be anticipated by all. Give all a chance to *be themselves*, to *express themselves* and to *govern themselves*. Let the groups grow into their parts until their action becomes full of rhythm and naturalness of expression. Retain only such gestures as are essential to the story and eliminate all that is false, pretentious or insincere. Some time ago a group of Italian girls participating in a festival of Yuletide customs in many lands, were asked to dramatize the old folk legend of Befana, the "gift-bearer" of Italian children. On the night the Lord Jesus was born, so goes the tale, the three Kings, laden with gifts of ointments, jewels and sweet oils, knocked at the Befana's door and asked her to accompany them in their quest for the Child of Bethlehem. The Befana, busy with her sweeping, could not be interrupted, however, and the Wise Men journeyed on alone. After finishing her sweeping, the Befana, taking her broom and a basket of sweetmeats for the Baby Jesus, started out for Bethlehem. But, alas, she had forgotten to ask the way of the old men and they had gone so far she could not overtake them. Throughout the centuries, therefore, the Befana has slipped down every chimney on Epiphany

TECHNIQUE OF PRODUCTION

Eve, in her vain search for the Christ Child. Modern Italian children regard the Befana with the greatest awe and are warned by their mothers that she "will fetch and eat them" if they are naughty. They prepare for her coming by hanging their clothes around the hearth after carefully emptying the pockets. All good children are rewarded with confections while those who are bad get only ashes or rods of birch.

Six bright-eyed, curly haired little girls were selected to prepare for the Befana's coming on Epiphany Eve. An older girl, somewhat dull and unresponsive, was chosen for the Befana. Before the spirit of the legend was caught, all were stiff and wooden in their actions. Gradually, however, the children forgot that they were acting; they forgot that they were being looked at; the Befana forgot her hands and feet; she was a very, very old woman; it hurt her to move; her back ached from endlessly stooping to fill so many pockets; truly it was wearisome for her to toil on through more than nineteen hundred years! Thus the old folk legend became revitalized during rehearsal periods. It was no longer regarded as a grandmother's fireside tale but became a real experience to the children themselves. So completely did they enter into the atmosphere of the story at its final presentation that the audience, composed of peoples from many lands, were enabled to share

TECHNIQUE OF PRODUCTION

understandingly and sympathetically something of the festal spirit of ancient Italy. Every national group should be rehearsed separately until dress rehearsals. Two dress rehearsals are advisable, although full make-up and properties are not necessary until the second. Have a period of four days to a week elapse between the first and second dress rehearsals in order to perfect the individual groups in details of acting and costuming. Two or three days should separate the second dress rehearsal from the final performance, so that actors and committee may get thoroughly rested. In some towns it will be found extremely difficult to have more than one final rehearsal, since many of the foreign people are engaged in night work. Although the director may herself be thoroughly disheartened by the bungling mistakes always made at dress rehearsals, she must on no account manifest her feelings. She must give encouragement or direction where needed, constructive criticism where there is failure to comprehend, and must, above all, preserve a calm presence and a humorous point of view.

Programs and Tickets

The programs should contain a simple résumé of the festival theme or story, since the action is portrayed through dance, song and pantomime in-

TECHNIQUE OF PRODUCTION

stead of through the spoken word. Make the program so complete in itself that anyone reading it will easily grasp the idea. List the *dramatis personae* according to national groups. Remember that a festival has no stars and that festival thinking is group thinking.

If the budget is limited, as is often the case, advertisements should be employed sufficient at least to cover the cost of printing. The interest of foreign banks, merchants, studios, schools and colleges should be solicited. You will find remarkable coöperation from such quarters and will be enabled to raise the desired amount with but little difficulty.

The matter of tickets brings up the question as to whether or not admission is to be charged. Actual demonstrations have shown that a large festival may be produced on an entirely self-supporting basis without asking an admission fee. No fixed rule can be applied as to charging admission since circumstances and conditions vary with each community. If the festival is given in the ideal sense, as a community enterprise free to all and for all, no charge should be made. If, on the other hand, it is necessary to raise money, tickets should be issued some weeks in advance of the performance. Patrons and patronesses may be secured, thus insuring additional interest and ticket sales. Whatever the sale price of

TECHNIQUE OF PRODUCTION

tickets, it is urgently advised that the cheaper ones come within easy reach of the hard-working foreigner, who will form a large and appreciative proportion of the audience.

PERFORMANCE ORGANIZATION.

Systematic performance organization is of greater importance to the success of the festival than any other one thing. Before the performance the director should post behind the scenes a chart showing the location and duties of the various chairmen, committees and national groups. Everyone should be required to report in the proper places two hours before the curtain rises.

Following is a performance organization outline which may be more or less expanded or modified according to the needs of a specific festival.

BEHIND THE SCENES:

1. *Dressing Room Signs and Monitors*

Every national group should have a dressing room or special section designated by a clear sign on which the name of the nationality and the number of its appearance on the program is printed. Every group is in charge of a nationality monitor who *remains with her group* from the time of arrival until all are ready to go home. The monitor is responsible for the conduct of her people, for taking them to make-up and inspection

TECHNIQUE OF PRODUCTION

rooms, for seeing that they are in the wings at the beginning of the episode preceding theirs, and for gathering together all costumes and accessories and presenting them to the costume chairman at the end of the performance.

2. *Make-Up*

Each national group is made up in order of its appearance on the program. As was previously said, the make-up chairman must provide a large enough committee to do the work quickly and efficiently. No talking or disorder should be permitted in the make-up room. The chairman provides scissors, absorbent cotton, surgical gauze, cleansing cream and soap, as well as make-up. The cotton and gauze are cut into individual squares so that each person may have fresh cotton for powder and rouge and gauze for cleansing. The make-up committee is responsible for cleaning up the participants after the performance, as well as for making them up. As soon as the groups are made up, the monitors conduct them to the costume director. The make-up room, as well as dressing and inspection rooms, must be clearly labeled.

3. *Costume Inspection*

The costume chairman carefully inspects each performer when dressed for the stage. She must be especially vigilant regarding the following fre-

TECHNIQUE OF PRODUCTION

quently neglected details: the uneven hanging of skirts, showing of petticoats, wrinkling of stockings, improper adjustment of kerchiefs, headdresses and bodices, the wearing of inappropriate jewelry and the untidy appearance of the hair. The costume chairman must be supplied with needles and thread, pins and shears so she may be armed against any disconcerting last-minute emergency.

4. *Final Inspection and Disposition of Cast*

After costume inspection, all are taken to the general director for a final examination. The director can often detect errors which pass unnoticed by her chairmen.

The question of what to do with the various groups until it is time for them to appear on the stage is perplexing to many directors. If the festival to be given is simple in character, it is sometimes possible to seat the cast in the first rows of the audience and have stage entrances and exits made in informal fashion from steps at either side of the front of the stage. This seating arrangement is much enjoyed by the participants, who are thus enabled to see those scenes in which they themselves do not appear.

Another plan is to have the cast seated in a reserved section of the balcony. Very competent monitors are needed in this case, to prevent mis-

TECHNIQUE OF PRODUCTION

takes in getting their groups quietly into the wings at the necessary time.

The third and only advisable plan where the festival produced is on a large scale, is to keep the cast away from the wings and out of sight of the audience until time for appearance on the stage. Much of the real festal spirit, so successfully preserved by the first method, is thus lost, but additional finish and more complete surprise to the audience is nevertheless obtained.

IN THE WINGS: A half hour before raising the curtain, everybody and everything in the wings should be in perfect readiness to begin. The stage manager and her assistants should be ready to give cues to the electrician and curtain man, and all properties must be in their proper places. The general director must be prepared for action wherever her services are most needed. If the stage set suggested at the beginning of the chapter is employed, the director should station competent helpers at each door of the set in order to insure easy entrances and exits. No more people than are necessary should be allowed in the wings and no whispering or laughing should be permitted, since all noise behind the scenes is noticeable from the audience.

WITH THE ORCHESTRA: The music director is stationed with the orchestra throughout the performance. She is responsible for all music cues

TECHNIQUE OF PRODUCTION

and should be quick-witted enough to have the orchestra supply appropriate additional music in case any unlooked-for gaps should occur in the action.

ON THE FLOOR: The chairman of business arrangements is responsible for selling and taking tickets at the door and checking the wraps of the audience. She should act as floor hostess, direct the ushers and the distribution of programs and see that all runs smoothly.

An additional festal touch may be added in the audience by having the ushers dressed in native peasant costumes. Flower and candy girls, also in costumes of other lands, may go up and down the aisles selling nosegays and European confections from gaily painted baskets.

GENERAL HINTS FOR THE DIRECTOR:

1. Begin the performance *on time*.
2. Never give a second performance if you can help it, since it will probably mean the loss of much spontaneity and freshness of action on the part of the performers.
3. See that every committee member, participant and stage hand is supplied with a program. " 'Tis pleasure sure to see one's name in print," and it is also easier to tell from a program where one's part comes in.
4. Be prepared for emergencies. They always

TECHNIQUE OF PRODUCTION

occur and must be met with calmness and quickness of thought and action.

5. If flags are to be used, employ flags of *all* the nations participating and not those of one or two countries. Race pride must be considered and respected.
6. Be conscientious about cleaning up after the festival. See that properties are returned to their rightful owners, costumes are carefully pressed and packed away, remaining make-up is saved and labeled and that everything is closed in an orderly fashion. Many a practical community object lesson may be learned from the manner in which you do or do not end the festival business.
7. Be generous with well-deserved praise to workers and cast after the performance. An informal festival party is a delightful way for a director to end her work and bring committee and cast together for the last time.

CHAPTER VI

FESTIVAL EXPERIMENTS IN FOREIGN COMMUNITIES

THE MCKEESPORT FOLK FESTIVAL OF EARLY SPRING

In May, 1922, the International Institute of McKeesport, Pennsylvania, made the interesting experiment of using an "Old World Folk Festival of Early Spring" as the means of welding together, for the first time, the foreign- and American-born of the city in a community undertaking. The demonstration proved extremely successful and the method followed in organizing and producing the festival was so practical that it may hold suggestions for other foreign workers. An outline of the festival is therefore given below, as well as the story of how it was developed in the community.

STAGE SETTING: At the outset of the undertaking the hearty interest and coöperation of the McKeesport National Tube Company were secured, who generously volunteered to furnish the material for the stage setting and to have it constructed by their expert workmen. The semicircular set

FESTIVAL EXPERIMENTS

measured forty feet across, and was similar in character to the one described at the beginning of Chapter V. Rain made it impossible to hold the festival out of doors, so the set had to be reduced on short notice to fit the indoor stage, which was only thirty-two feet across. The Tube Company sent men and a truck to the hills to gather green boughs and branches, which were woven through the lattice background and hung over the doors. Brilliant paper flowers were fastened carelessly among the leaves, thus effecting the illusion of a row of charming peasant cottages in early spring.

THE FESTIVAL: After a preliminary program of well-executed exercises and drills by various local foreign athletic societies and groups, the festival proper, consisting of European folk customs of early spring, was given. The first episode represented "Carrying Death from the Village." Winter, the bringer of ill luck, sickness and misfortune, has become associated with death in the peasant mind. Winter, or Death, represented by a black-draped bier, was therefore carried from the village by a group of Slovak and Uhro-Rusin men, women and children marching with measured tread to the strains of a funeral march played by the Hungarian Gypsy Orchestra. An old peasant with long white beard and bent back followed

FESTIVAL EXPERIMENTS

the villagers and sang at length the mournful Slovak melody, *Ja som baca, vel'mi stary* (I am a very old man).[1]

In the next scene, "Bringing in Summer," rejoicing took the place of mourning. The return of Summer, heralded by the village folk with merrymaking and song, was symbolized by the May Queen, the bough of green, May gifts and the dance about the Maypole. A group of stately Hungarian maidens in full white skirts and red velvet bodices trimmed with gold braid were led into the village by their lovely white-clad queen. After crowning her with a wreath of white roses, the girls danced the Magyar *Kör* (Circle) Dance[2] with characteristic grace and skill.

Polish girls with primly braided hair and brightly colored bodices decked their May boughs with gay ribbons, singing meanwhile *Gaiczek zielony* (The Green Grove).[3] Then, with prettily decorated boughs, they went singing from door to door in the village and received cakes and flowers. Thus the children dramatized the words of their old spring folk song:

[1] Slovak songs obtained through the courtesy of M. Paul Jamarik, chief elder of Young Folks' Circle, National Slovak Society, Pittsburgh, Pa.
[2] Music of *Ritka, buza,* in Folk Songs of Many Peoples, by F. H. Botsford, Vol. 1, p. 172.
[3] *Ibid.,* Vol. 1, p. 60.

FESTIVAL EXPERIMENTS

> To their house, if you came,
> They'd greet you in Jesus' name;
> He in rich embroideries,
> She with cap and jingling keys;
> Both will surely have a gift for us;
> They are rich and kind and generous.

After making the rounds of the village, the children joined in a vigorous dance of folk origin.

The Slovaks welcomed the return of summer with boisterous gaiety. Some of the women, carrying baskets of flowers and cookies, showered their favors on orchestra and audience and sang their jolly little Slovak folk songs, *Majálesová* (Come on, boys, May is here)[1] and *Jáhody, cernice, maliny* (Blackberries, raspberries, strawberries).[1]

The welcome of summer was completed by a group of American children who performed the time-honored custom of weaving the Maypole.

The return of summer was not undisputed, however, for the ever watchful Winter King, with his attendant sprites, was unwilling to give up his land without a struggle. Hence the "Conflict of Summer and Winter" took place.

The lights on the stage were turned low and Summer and her flower attendants fell into a deep slumber. Then a tiny brownie bearing a lantern

[1] Slovak songs obtained through the courtesy of M. Paul Jamarik, chief elder of Young Folks' Circle, National Slovak Society, Pittsburgh, Pa.

FESTIVAL EXPERIMENTS

appeared and, peering into the faces of the drowsing blossoms, wakened them one by one. Summer waved her wand over the flowers and marshaled her forces to meet the white-clad Winter King, who was seen approaching with his frost sprites from the opposite side. A battle of rhyming couplets of old folk origin ensued. After Summer and her followers had sung the last lines, a fierce battle of flowers and snowballs (white rubber balloons) followed. Winter's mantle was captured and with his attendants he was chased far into the woods. Summer and her flowers danced triumphantly and the assembled nationalities expressed their joy over Winter's final departure by characteristic folk songs and dances.

Italian girls in brilliant costumes danced the *Tarantella* and sang *O sole mio* and *O Maria, mari*. The festival ended with two tiny Hungarian children's dancing "Comin' through the Rye."

The real success of the festival lay not so much in the skill of the performers, the picturesqueness of the vivid peasant costumes and the charm of the stage setting as in the fact that all the participants had a good time and that each and every one of the actors was radiant with the spirit of youth and joy and eternal spring. By working together on a community festival, racial differences were forgotten, petty prejudices were wiped

FESTIVAL EXPERIMENTS

away, and many Americans came to understand, for the first time, perhaps, something of the beauty brought to their midst by the large foreign population dwelling among them.

COSTUMING AND THE COMMUNITY WORKSHOP: The budget of the McKeesport Institute left no margin for festival expenses, hence costuming, properties, advertising and other items had to be planned on the lowest possible scale. The problem of costuming was, therefore, a serious one for a cast numbering about a hundred and twenty. The following arrangements were finally made: The Hungarian group, consisting of eight girls, bought the material and made their own costumes under the supervision of the Hungarian Institute worker. These costumes represented hours of painstaking labor and were authentic in every detail. Italian, Polish and some Slovak costumes were borrowed from a distance. Other Slovak costumes were made with the help of beautiful old shawls, headdresses and aprons hunted out by the foreign women from chests and closets at home.

The administrative office of the Institute was temporarily turned into a community workshop where women of many different nationalities, including Hungarians, Slovaks, Croatians and Americans, came to make the rest of the costumes and the stage properties. This part of the work

FESTIVAL EXPERIMENTS

was largely under the direction of a French milliner possessing rare skill and artistic ability, who volunteered her expert services. Old muslin underslips and shirts were lent by the Croatian children as foundations for the frost and flower costumes in the "Conflict" scene. Realistic frost sprite costumes with tall icicle caps were made for the boys, while the girls had exquisite dresses and caps of pastel shades representing roses, daffodils, forget-me-nots and other flowers. The material used was Dennison's crêpe paper. The cost of the twelve costumes amounted to $3.84 and they were later bought back by the children at thirty-five cents each. The effect of these costumes was charming and called forth great admiration from all who saw them. Many foreign mothers came to the workshop and deftly made paper flowers, costumes and properties. Many spoke but little English and oftentimes the work had to be explained through signs and gestures.

MUSIC: The music for the festival represented the finest talent of local foreign musicians, who donated many dollars' worth of time and services to the cause. The director of the Croatian Tambourica Orchestra composed special music for the "Conflict of Summer and Winter," orchestrated several of the foreign folk songs and left his business for rehearsals and for the final festival. The leader of the Italian band came day after day to rehearse with the various groups and sat up the most of one night in order to arrange some of the music. The Hungarian Gypsy Orchestra played with a wild abandon which inspired audience and performers. Although some of the foreign orchestras had complained that they had to play too much even when paid for their music at entertainments, no lack of enthusiasm or unwillingness to play was noticeable in the unstinted service they volunteered for the community festival.

REHEARSALS: Rehearsals were periods of good fellowship and sociability to the various foreign groups. Strict attention and keen interest were shown and one group often stimulated another to greater originality or dramatic action. For instance, the Polish children, after seeing the beautiful Hungarian dance at dress rehearsal, whispered in the director's ear that they "knew a dance, too," which they diligently practiced and gave at the final performance. The Croatian children so loved to rehearse that disappointment, and almost mutiny, were visible on their faces when they were informed that further rehearsals were unnecessary. Some of the mothers and helpers came to rehearsals and assisted in many ways.

COMMUNITY COOPERATION: Besides making the stage set and granting the services of its men

FESTIVAL EXPERIMENTS

for that purpose, the National Tube Company allowed the members of the Croatian Tambourica Orchestra, employed by them on night shift, time off on three evenings in order to rehearse for the festival, and promised to furnish ushers and lights for the performance if given out of doors as originally planned. Local banks and merchants, at the solicitation of interested Americans, gave forty dollars' worth of advertisements to meet the cost of programs and other festival expenses. One of the moving-picture houses had slides made at a cost of sixty cents to advertise the festival and these slides were shown at each of four local picture theatres. Foreign and American private individuals donated quantities of fresh flowers from their gardens, selected costume materials and acted as dressers, assistants in the make-up room and general helpers at the time of the festival. The school auditorium where the entertainment was held was rented at a minimum fee. Thus the whole community shared in making the festival a success.

The story of the McKeesport festival is characteristic of other festivals given in small country towns or valley districts, where hamlets, towns and cities have come together in the interest of a community undertaking. Everywhere the festival has tended to create a bond of brotherhood between races separated widely by religious and political belief, to establish a greater respect for the beauty and symbolism of Old Country rites, and to teach the younger generation of American birth a more sincere love for the colorful background from which it has sprung.

Festivals Tried and Proven

Because of the great lack of festal material available to foreign community workers, and because successful festivals are the outgrowth of actual experience and not the fruit of poetic musing, the seasonal festival outlines in the succeeding chapters have been compiled, in the hope that they may prove useful to those believing that the festival is more and more becoming a means of aesthetic approach to our friends from other lands.

The following festivals have, in many cases, been demonstrated in American cities and communities having a predominating foreign population. They are the result of a careful study of the home customs and oral traditions of many races. In some instances a somewhat symbolic interpretation of certain customs has been given for the sake of obtaining greater unity of dramatic action; everywhere, however, faithfulness and loyalty to the true spirit of the European folk festival has been conscientiously observed.

The suggested festivals may be used either in

their entirety, or in part. The number of participants is unlimited, and customs of countries not already included in the festival texts may be introduced according to the needs of a given community. For this reason, appendices have been supplied, in which additional peasant customs, suitable to the individual requirements of the outlined festivals, have been included. At the beginning of each festival a repetition of technical details of stage setting has been risked, in order that the reader may not be forced continually to turn back to the general information on stage settings outlined in Chapter V. It is perhaps needless to say that an ideal stage setting has in every case been suggested. Simpler arrangements will oftentimes have to be made, according to varying circumstances in different communities.

THE TRIUMPH OF SPRING
A Festival of Old World Songs and Ceremonial Rites

THE TRIUMPH OF SPRING
PRODUCTION NOTES

STAGE SETTING

The set is semicircular in form and measures forty feet across. A wooden lattice twelve feet high, with five doors two and one-half by nine feet inserted at regular intervals, forms the background. The doors are made by stretching muslin or canvas over wooden frames and are painted pale green or yellow. They open outward toward the audience and are arranged with fastenings on the inner side. Fragrant spring boughs and branches are woven through the lattice background between and over the doors. Gaily colored crêpe paper vines and blossoms are fastened here and there among the green. The general effect produced is of a row of village cottages in early spring. One-third of the distance across the stage, between the first and second doors at the left, stands an octagonal gray stone well, four feet high by three feet across, over which an artificial dogwood tree, ten feet high, droops its branches.

No curtain is needed between the episodes, as all scenery shifts are made on the stage by children in Old World costumes.

Costuming and Properties

"National Costumes of the Slavic Peoples," published by The Womans Press, New York, 1920, price $2.00, gives excellent practical suggestions for making Slavic costumes. The following numbers of the *National Geographic Magazine* will prove extremely helpful in planning costumes for the countries indicated:

Czecho-Slovakia—Dec. 1918, Vol. 34, pp. 491-4; Feb. 1921, Vol. 39, pp. 120-55; Feb. 1923, Vol. 43, pp. 157-60.
Germany—Feb. 1923, Vol. 43, pp. 153-7.
Hungary—Dec. 1918, Vol. 34, pp. 485, 495-6, 498-500; Feb. 1923, Vol. 43, pp. 162, 165, 167.
Ireland—April 1915, Vol. 27, pp. 401-8; Dec. 1915, Vol. 28, pp. 551-3, 555; Dec. 1918, Vol. 34, p. 526; Feb. 1923, Vol. 43, p. 180.
Italy—June 1915, Vol. 27, p. 613; Nov. 1915, Vol. 28, pp. 446-9; Oct. 1916, Vol. 30, pp. 298-301, 313, 342, 346, 350-9; Feb. 1923, Vol. 43, pp. 181-96.
Poland—Feb. 1923, Vol. 43, p. 161.
Serbia—April 1915, Vol. 27, pp. 419, 425-32; Oct. 1915, Vol. 28, p. 389; Dec. 1918, Vol. 34, p. 474; Aug. 1919, Vol. 36, p. v.

Authentic colored prints illustrating the national costumes, folk festivals and customs of many races may be obtained from twenty-five cents upward through Rudolf Lesch, 225 Fifth Avenue, New York City. Scandinavian prints

THE TRIUMPH OF SPRING

may be purchased from thirty-five cents upward through Albert Bonnier, 561 Third Avenue, New York City.

The costumes worn in Part III by Spring and the flowers, as well as those of the Winter King and frost sprites, should be made from crêpe paper, since the effect produced under artificial light is of greater delicacy and tonal softness than is obtainable from other materials. The well, dogwood tree and artificial flowers may all be fashioned from crêpe paper. Free charts and working instructions for costumes and stage properties will be furnished upon written request to the Dennison Manufacturing Company, Service Department, Fifth Avenue and Twenty-sixth Street, New York City.

Folk Songs and Dances

FOLK SONGS OF MANY PEOPLES, with English versions by American poets, by F. H. Botsford. 2 Vols., The Womans Press, New York, 1921-2. Price $2.75 and $3.50.

FOLK DANCES AND SINGING GAMES, by Elizabeth Burchenal. Schirmer, New York, 1909. Price $1.50.

FOLK DANCES FROM OLD HOMELANDS, by Elizabeth Burchenal. Schirmer, New York, 1922. Price $1.50.

FOLK DANCES AND GAMES, by Caroline Crawford. Barnes, New York, 1909. Price $1.50.

POPULAR FOLK GAMES AND DANCES, by M. R. Hofer. Flanagan, Chicago, 1907. Price $.75.

THE TRIUMPH OF SPRING

Programs

It is suggested that the programs be printed in the three sections indicated by Parts I, II and III. The names of the various nations, with the accompanying italicized description of the customs, should appear on the program, so that the festival theme may be clearly understood by those not already possessing knowledge of European peasant life and customs.

OUTLINE OF FESTIVAL

PART I

May Day Eve Preparations

IRELAND

According to an ancient Irish folk belief, on May Day Eve all thresholds must be strewn with marsh marigolds as a charm against evil fairies seeking on that night to enter the homes to do harm. The first person coming to the house after the ceremony tramples on the flowers to insure the family good luck and plenty of butter throughout the year.

An aged Irish woman with snow white hair and bent back enters the stage through the middle right door. In one hand she carries a basket of marsh marigolds and in the other a cane. In passing from door to door, she scatters flowers on

THE TRIUMPH OF SPRING

every threshold, singing meanwhile the following charm. At the last words, she pauses to make the sign of the cross before entering the door.

Marigold Charm Song[1]

On this mystic Eve of May
Fairies come, so good folk say,
But I'll drive them far away
With my flowers.

May the stranger on his way
Trample down my flowers gay,
Bringing good luck every day
And happy hours.

May my butter yellow be
As the flowers now I see,
And evil distant flee
From every door.

On the night bad fairies come,
When my magic charm is sung,
May they leave me, one by one,
Forever more!

GERMANY

In certain parts of Germany it was customary on this Eve for village boys and girls to clean the wells so that they might have pure water throughout the season. Sometimes lanterns, hung in the trees, lighted the young people through their long night vigil beside the wells.

[1] Modern words by author to music of The Snowy-Breasted Pearl in Folk Songs of Many Peoples, Vol. 2, pp. 107-9.

THE TRIUMPH OF SPRING

Boys and girls, coming from different houses in the village, gather about the well where they busily remove sticks and stones from the water. While working, they hum and sing snatches of the old German folk song, "There Is a Reaper," in Folk Songs of Many Peoples, Vol. 2, pp. 164-5. The stage gradually grows dim to denote approaching night. The boys hang lighted lanterns in the tree. Some slumber on the ground or against the well, while others keep watch. As the moonlight suddenly floods the stage, one lad sings softly:

> How quiet is the moonrise!
> *Blue, blue blossom*
> She steals through silver clouded skies,
> *Rose garden flowers, maidens in towers,*
> O fairest Rosa.[1]

The stage grows lighter, the joyous note of the cuckoo is heard in the distance, and boys and girls awaken to partake in the May Day festivities.

The action between the German scene at the end of Part I and that at the beginning of Part II should be easy and continuous.

PART II

Bringing Spring into the Village

The return of spring, heralded by the village

[1] Folk Songs of Many Peoples, Vol. 2, pp. 169-70.

THE TRIUMPH OF SPRING

folk with merrymaking and rejoicing, is symbolized by the well festival (*Maibrunnenfeste*), the May Queen, the bough of green and the planting of the garlanded tree. The various races welcome spring after the fashion of their own countries.

GERMANY

At dawn of the first of May, village boys and girls were wont to rise, gather fresh flowers from the mountains and twine them into wreaths as well decorations. Eggs, symbolizing fertility, were placed among the flowers. The festival ended with dancing and song.

Young people, carrying baskets of flowers, join those who are keeping the night vigil. Together they fashion wreaths and place them around the well. Joining hands, they sing and dance "Twining the Wreath," in Popular Folk Games and Dances, p. 34.

HUNGARY

The village girls crown their white-clad queen with a wreath of lilies and dance with her the Magyar Kör (Circle) Dance.

The girls, led by their queen, enter rhythmically to the music of "Rare the Barley," in Folk Songs of Many Peoples, Vol. 1, pp. 172-3. Facing the audience, in semicircular arrangement with the queen in the centre, one girl performs the crowning ceremony and afterward all join in the Magyar *Kör* (Circle) Dance, *Csárdás* No. 2, in Folk Dances and Singing Games, pp. 60-4.

POLAND

Boys and girls decorate branches with gay ribbons and then go singing from door to door begging for gifts of money, eggs or cakes. The households giving presents are favored with a twig of green and are thought to share in the blessings of the spirit watching over crops and animals.

The boys and girls are greeted at the various doorways by men and women in peasant costumes standing within. They sing the "Green Grove," in Folk Songs of Many Peoples, Vol. 1, pp. 60-1. Later they dance the *Krakoviak*, in Popular Folk Games and Dances, p. 44, or the *Cracoviac*, in Folk Dances from Old Homelands, pp. 48-50.

ITALY

In certain Italian villages, the boys plant a garland-trimmed pine before the door of the most beautiful girl in the town.

After the planting, boys and girls dance the *Tarantella*, in Folk Dances and Singing Games, pp. 86-9.

THE TRIUMPH OF SPRING

JAPAN

Spring is the time of rejoicing to lovers in the East as well as in the West.

Two Japanese lovers trip across the stage, hand in hand, singing as they pass:

> With you, dear heart, when I journey,
> I care not how seasons pass,
> *Ho-cho-say, ho-cho-say!*
> O hear the nightingales call,
> It is spring, the spring,
> *Ho-cho-say, ho-cho-say!*[1]

As the lovers disappear, the stage grows dim, as if with approaching evening. Spring with her flowers enters singing *Mugur Mugurel* (in English) in Folk Songs of Many Peoples, Vol. 2, pp. 341-2. Spring and her attendants rest near the well and are soon overcome with sleep. In the stillness that follows, the dismal hooting of the owl is heard.

The transition between Parts II and III should be natural and easy.

PART III

Final Conflict of Spring and Winter

The return of Spring to the village is not undisputed, for the ever watchful Winter King with his attendant sprites is unwilling to give up his land

[1] Folk Songs of Many Peoples, Vol. 2, pp. 429-30.

THE TRIUMPH OF SPRING

without a struggle. Spring marshals her flowers to meet Winter, who descends upon her with little warning. The representatives of Spring and Winter exchange song couplets of traditional origin. Spring asks Winter to leave the land and Winter refuses. Finally they resort to a battle of flowers and snowballs. Winter's mantle is captured and he and his followers are chased into the woods. Spring and her attendants dance triumphantly about the mantle, which they bury under flowers.

At the foreboding hoot of the owl, Spring wakens and calls together her flowers. The Winter King, in icicle costume and long white mantle, accompanied by his frost sprites, rushes upon Spring. A combat of singing couplets[1] follows. As Spring and the flowers sing their verses, they step forward toward Winter in rhythm with the music. Winter and his sprites simultaneously step backward as if frightened. The reverse action takes place when Winter and his sprites

[1] The music for the couplets was composed by J. A. Ivcevich, director of the Croatian Tambourica Orchestra of McKeesport, Pennsylvania, for the McKeesport Festival, May 1922. The source of the couplets is found in J. G. Frazer, The Golden Bough, Vol. 2, pp. 100-101, 2d ed., Macmillan, London, 1900, 3 Vols. The author has taken the liberty of making slight adaptations in the original custom as well as in the couplet text in order to gain greater dramatic unity for the present festival.

THE TRIUMPH OF SPRING

sing their parts. Spring waves a flower wand as she sings and Winter threatens her with an icicle sceptre.

SPRING

WINTER

Spring

Green, green are meadows wherever we pass,
And the mowers are busy in the grass.

Winter

White, white are the meadows, wherever we go,
And the sledges glide hissing 'cross the snow.

Spring

We'll climb up the tree where the red cherries glow
And Winter can stand by himself down below.

Winter

With you we will climb the cherry tree tall
Its branches will kindle the fire in the hall.

THE TRIUMPH OF SPRING

Spring

We are the Springtime in bright array,
We're chasing the Winter far, far away.

Winter

We are the Winter in mantle of furs
We're chasing the Spring o'er bushes and burs.

Spring

Just say a word more, and we'll have you banned
At once and forever from Springtime's land.

Winter

O Spring, for all your bluster and brag,
You'd not dare to carry a hen in a bag.

Spring

O Winter, your chatter no more can we stay,
We'll kick and we'll cuff you without delay.

Here ensues the battle of flowers and snowballs. Handfuls of fresh flowers are thrown by Spring's attendants and white, frosted balloons, attached to fine threads which are broken at this point, are hurled by the frost sprites. At last Winter's mantle is captured and he and the sprites are driven far away. The cuckoo's call is once more heard and Spring and the flowers dance and sing the "Swiss May Dance," in Popular Folk Games and Dances, p. 35. Substitute the word "flowers" for "children" in text.

THE TRIUMPH OF SPRING

APPENDIX

Additional Customs for Substitution in Spring Festival

PART I

SWEDEN

On Valborg's Mess Eve (*May Day Eve*) *picnics are held in the open. Bonfires are lighted on the hills in the belief that their heat will drive away the Winter sprites.*

The villagers, coming from their cottages with baskets of luncheon, meet together for a jolly outing. If the festival is held out of doors, a bonfire is built at the right centre of the stage. As the lights grow dim to denote approaching dusk, all join in dancing around the bonfire the *Bleking*, in Folk Dances and Games, pp. 20-1.

PART II

CZECHO-SLOVAKIA

On Easter Monday the boys plait willow wands and ornament them with bright ribbons. With these they switch the girls "so they won't be lazy or have fleas," and every victim is obliged to give an egg to her tormentor.

The village lads meet on the green to fashion

THE TRIUMPH OF SPRING

their wands. A group of girls, seemingly unconscious of the boys' presence, draw water from the well. The prettiest girl, who stands somewhat apart from the rest, is greeted by one of the boys with the song:

> Andulko, thou my dearest,
> My joy, my bliss thou art,
> Andulko, ever nearest,
> Thou'rt my sweetheart, etc.[1]

Andulko shyly looks at the singer, then rushes through the nearest doorway and slams the door. The boys begin to chase the girls around the stage and they in turn are finally forced to present the boys with eggs. As the last girl gives up her egg, she sings:

> Boy, I adore you
> My golden laddie.
> Boy, I adore you,
> Honza, my lad.[2]

When the song is completed, Honza and his sweetheart run off the stage hand in hand.

Decorated Czecho-Slovak eggs and postcards illustrating Easter customs may be purchased through the Czecho-Slovak Art Shop, 328 East 72d Street, New York City.

[1] Folk Songs of Many Peoples, Vol. 1, pp. 134-5.
[2] Ibid., Vol. 1, p. 141.

THE TRIUMPH OF SPRING

SERBIA

On Cvijeti, *the Day of Flowers, the village folk go to the river bank to gather willows or grass. With these and church banners, they parade through the streets of the town.*

The village procession consists of men, women and children who wind across the stage to the music of the "Serbian National Anthem," in Folk Songs of Many Peoples, Vol. 1, pp. 210-11. This music is singularly appropriate, since *Cvijeti* is considered as more or less a national holiday by the Serbian people.

THE EVE OF ST. JOHN
A Midsummer Festival of Dance and Song

THE EVE OF ST. JOHN

PRODUCTION NOTES

STAGE SETTING

The midsummer festival must be given out of doors to be most effective.

The set is semicircular in form and measures forty feet across. A wooden lattice, twelve feet high, with three doors two and one-half by nine feet inserted in the centre front of the latticework and midway between the centre front and either edge, forms the background. The doors are made by stretching muslin or canvas over wooden frames and are painted yellow and decorated with gay Slavic designs in red, green and blue. The doors open outward toward the audience, and are arranged with convenient fastenings on the inner side. Green boughs and branches are woven through the lattice background, between and over the doors. Tall birch branches or small trees with sharpened trunks are stuck into the ground at irregular intervals against the background.

No curtain is needed between the episodes as the scenery shifts are made by children in Old World costumes.

Costuming

"National Costumes of the Slavic Peoples," published by The Womans Press, New York, 1920, price $2.00, gives excellent practical suggestions for making Slavic costumes.

The following numbers of the *National Geographic Magazine* will prove extremely helpful in planning costumes for the countries indicated:

Czecho-Slovakia—Dec. 1918, Vol. 34, pp. 491-4; Feb. 1921, Vol. 39, pp. 120-55; Feb. 1923, Vol. 43, pp. 157-60.

France—Nov. 1915, Vol. 28, pp. 392-3, 411-32, 435, 451-4; Nov. 1917, Vol. 32, p. 508; Dec. 1918, Vol. 34, p. 525; July 1921, Vol. 40, pp. 29-44; Feb. 1923, Vol. 43, pp. 149-60.

Italy—June 1915, Vol. 27, p. 613; Nov. 1915, Vol. 28, pp. 446-9; Oct. 1916, Vol. 30, pp. 298-301, 313, 342, 346, 350-9; Feb. 1923, Vol. 43, pp. 181-96.

Latvia—Feb. 1923, Vol. 43, p. 176.

Russia—July 1917, Vol. 32, p. 85; Sept. 1917, Vol. 32, p. 239.

Authentic colored prints illustrating the national costumes, folk festivals and customs of different lands may be obtained from twenty-five cents upward through Rudolf Lesch, 225 Fifth Avenue, New York City. Scandinavian prints may be purchased from thirty-five cents upward through Albert Bonnier, 561 Third Avenue, New York City.

THE EVE OF ST. JOHN

Properties

MAYPOLE: The Scandinavian Maypole needed for the last episode differs greatly from the Maypoles with which we are familiar in this country. A print entitled The Maypole Dance, by Anders Zorn, should be sent for through either of the above mentioned dealers, in order that the character of the pole, or "tree" as it is called, may be clearly understood. A strong slender tree, ten or eleven feet high, is stripped of all its leaves and of all but two horizontal branches about three feet from the top. From these branches, at an equal distance from the trunk, two large wreaths of field flowers are hung. A bunch of gay posies tied with bright ribbons crowns the top of the tree. No ribbon streamers are used.

BONFIRES: As the bonfires are built on the stage in the presence of the audience, their construction and the time spent in their burning should be carefully rehearsed. Fir, pine and balsam mixed with dry kindlings may be rapidly laid and are quickly consumed when ignited. It will be noted that no bonfires are used until the last two episodes. The participants must be warned to exercise the greatest possible care in dancing around them. Adults instead of children should be chosen for these dances.

GARLANDS AND WREATHS: The garlands of the Lettish episode are fashioned of blue corn-

THE EVE OF ST. JOHN

flowers, yellow camomile (feverfew), yellow and white daisies, red clover and oak leaves. The wreaths with which the villagers are crowned consist of oak leaves and flowers. Patterns and complete directions for making flowers and leaves will be furnished upon written request to the Dennison Manufacturing Company, Service Department, Fifth Avenue and Twenty-sixth Street, New York City.

TORCHES: If great precaution against fire is observed by the men carrying the torches, they may be most effectively made from tar barrels, according to the Lettish custom. Small tar barrels three by two feet are filled with pitch, ignited and raised on tall poles, thus forming great torches visible through the night for a long distance. In case smaller and safer torches are desirable, tin cans may be filled with pitch, fastened to poles and waved aloft.

FIREFLIES: Small "bug lights" or electric flashlights, purchasable at an electric supply company for about twenty-five cents each, are ideal for fireflies when flashed from the hands of the dancers. Fireflies may be more cheaply represented by small discs of pasteboard dipped in phosphorescent paint. These discs are in the hands of the dancers as they enter and are tossed and caught throughout the dance.

THE EVE OF ST. JOHN

FERN BLOSSOM: The mystical red fern blossom for the Russian episode is represented by a red electric light bulb hidden in an embankment of ferns at the base of one of the trees at the right of the stage.

Folk Songs and Dances

FOLK SONGS OF MANY PEOPLES, with English versions by American poets, by F. H. Botsford. 2 Vols. The Womans Press, New York. 1921-2. Price $2.75 and $3.50.

FOLK DANCES AND SINGING GAMES, by Elizabeth Burchenal. Schirmer, New York, 1909. Price $1.50.

FOLK DANCES FROM OLD HOMELANDS, by Elizabeth Burchenal. Schirmer, New York, 1922. Price $1.50.

FOLK DANCES AND GAMES, by Caroline Crawford. Barnes, New York, 1909. Price $1.50.

POPULAR FOLK GAMES AND DANCES, by M. R. Hofer. Flanagan, Chicago, 1907. Price $1.50.

Duration of Performance

About an hour and three-quarters.

Programs

The names of the various nations, together with the italicized descriptions of the midsummer customs, should appear on the program, so that the festival theme may be clearly understood by those not already possessing knowledge of European peasant life and customs.

THE EVE OF ST. JOHN

OUTLINE OF FESTIVAL
LATVIA

Fragrant birch trees and gaily hued flowers are gathered from mountain sides and fashioned into arches before the village houses. Young and old, wreathed with oak leaves and field flowers, walk in vivid procession to the master's house, bearing gifts and singing songs especially composed for the occasion. Immense torches, or St. John's fires, lighted and waved aloft, illumine the merry revel of feasting, dancing and singing.

Boys and men laden with young birch trees busily make arches of green for each of the village houses. The arches are formed by driving sharpened tree trunks into the ground at a distance of about a foot from the doorways and two and one-half feet apart. The trees are about nine feet high and the upper branches are tied together in the middle, thus forming an archway. Holes for the trunks must be made beforehand and the construction of the arches must be so thoroughly rehearsed that the work on the stage can progress rapidly without loss of interest on the part of the audience. While the men are thus engaged, women and girls sit about in picturesque groups, adding the finishing touches to long garlands of field flowers. As the work progresses the men and girls sing alternately:

THE EVE OF ST. JOHN

Men: Where have you been growing, my sweet?
Maid, why did we never meet?
Maid, why did we never meet?
Ri di la la!

Girls: I was in a garden growing
Where the roses flourished, too,
Where the roses flourished, too,
Ri di la la![1]

When the decoration of the houses is completed, all leave the stage through the doors at right and left. In a moment the villagers reënter in processional formation. All are crowned with festive wreaths. The girls and women carry in their aprons such offerings as grasses, field flowers and cheeses wrapped in cloths. The procession winds slowly across the stage singing the *Ligo,* the endless song of greeting. All stop before the arch in the centre of the stage and are heartily welcomed by the master and his wife who stand within and give cakes, beer and sweetmeats to their guests in return for the offerings. The stage lights are turned low, torches are lighted and the scene ends with merrymaking and drinking to the master's health.

[1] Folk Songs of Many Peoples, Vol. 1, p. 28.

THE EVE OF ST. JOHN

THE EVE OF ST. JOHN

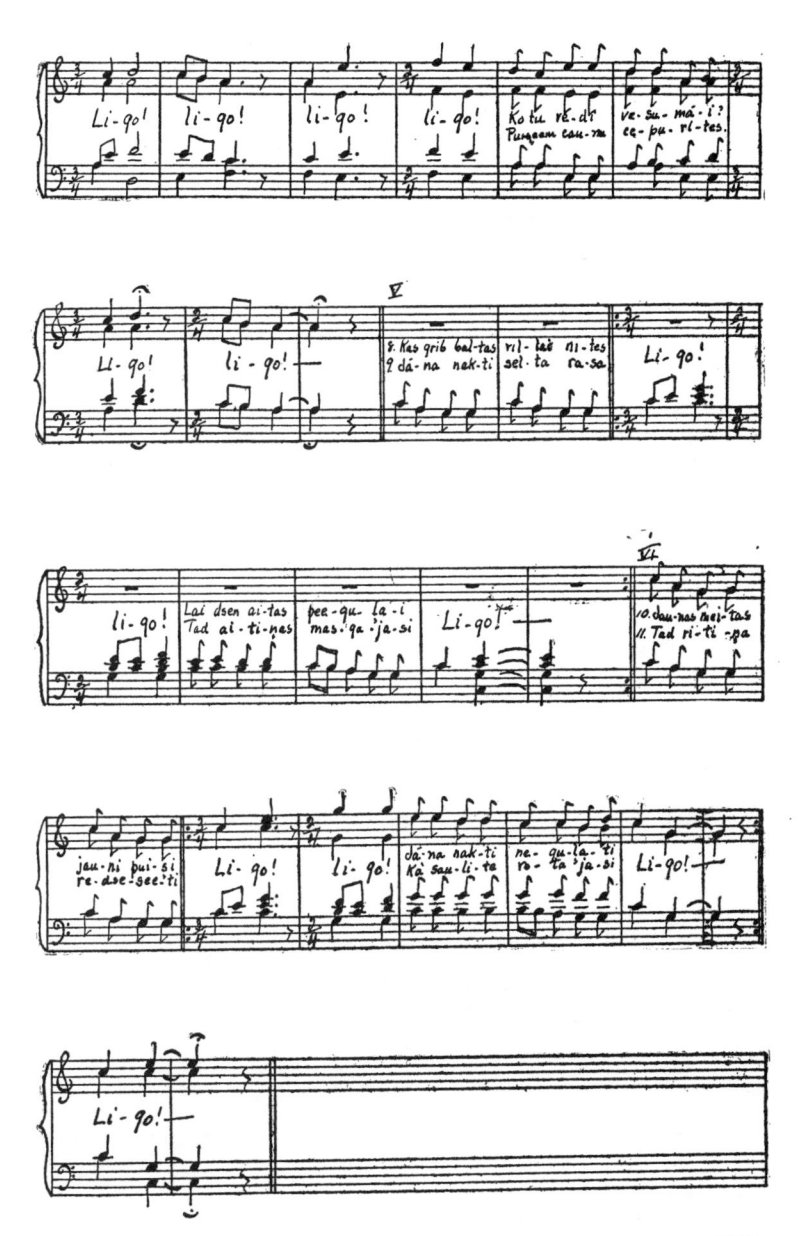

THE EVE OF ST. JOHN

Ligo Song[1]

Only once a year came Johnny,
    Ligo! ligo!
Visiting his little children.
    Ligo! ligo! ligo!
Visiting his little children.
    Ligo!

How they ate and how they drank then,
    Ligo! ligo!
Loudly singing Johnny's praises.
    Etc.[2]

O, good evening, Johnny's mother,
    Ligo! ligo!
Did you not expect to see us?
    Etc.

She has tied soft cheese in bundles,
    Ligo! ligo!
And sweet beer has brewed us, also.
    Etc.

Beer, good beer, then, Johnny's father,
    Ligo! ligo!
Barley in your field is growing.
    Etc.

Hi now, Johnny, God's own sonny,
    Ligo! ligo!
What have you there in your wagon?
    Etc.

[1] English version by Helen Jauncey Kingsbury.
[2] The three "ligo's" and the second line of each stanza are repeated.

THE EVE OF ST. JOHN

Beaded chains I bring for maidens;
  Ligo! ligo!
For the youths are caps of sable.
  Etc.

She who wants a small white plaidie,
  Ligo! ligo!
Must drive out her sheep at evening.
  Etc.

St. John's Eve brings dew that's golden,
  Ligo! ligo!
And your sheep should all be washed then.
  Etc.

O you lads, and O you lasses,
  Ligo! ligo!
Do not sleep on St. John's evening.
  Etc.

Then you'll see in early morning
  Ligo! ligo!
How the little sun rejoices.
  Etc.

BELGIUM

Good luck will be the lot of those catching glow-worms on the Eve of St. John.

Merry groups of peasant folk enter the stage, right and left, to the music of "The Little Sheep Girl," in Folk Songs of Many Peoples, Vol. 2, p. 139. The two groups wind rhythmically in circular formation around both sides of the stage,

THE EVE OF ST. JOHN

alternately walking and waltzing in time with the music, and showing the fireflies as they dance. Just as the dance is completed a sturdy villager enters through the centre door and begins singing, as all crowd around to listen:

> Now all draw near and hear from me
> The tale of Pierlala;
> A gay young scalawag was he,
> The joy of his papa.
> He laughed and joked the whole day long,
> His life was like this merry song,
> The tale of Pierlala, sa, sa!
> The tale of Pierlala.[1]

The crowd constantly shifts during the song and merry laughter forms a fitting conclusion to each verse.

CZECHO-SLOVAKIA

Herbs, gathered on St. John's Eve, are believed by the peasants to possess rare medicinal virtues.

Brightly kerchiefed women and children with baskets on their arms search for herbs around the roots of the trees. A gaudily attired native farmer struts across the stage while the herb plucking is going on, and all burst out singing:

> Sedlák, Sedlák, Sedlák
> Struts like an old peacock;
> Sedlák, Sedlák, Sedlák

[1] Folk Songs of Many Peoples, Vol. 2, pp. 140-1.

THE EVE OF ST. JOHN

Of high estate;
Round about his waist a belt,
'Broidered on his coat of pelt,
Tuli, tuli, tuli, tulips ornate.[1]

Sedlák rushes angrily at the singers, who scatter in every direction. The village youths come strolling by and all join in the picturesque "Handkerchief Dance," in Folk Dances from Old Homelands, pp. 73-4.

FRANCE (Brittany)

Bonfires are built on every hillside. Peasants in holiday attire dance all night to the accompaniment of the shepherd's horn. A superstition exists that girls dancing around nine fires before midnight will be married within the year.

Three bonfires are built in triangular formation in the middle of the stage. The fire at the point of the triangle nearest the audience is at the outer edge of the stage, directly in the centre. Sufficient space must be allowed around each fire to permit dancing without danger to full skirts. The couples dance nine times around every bonfire *Jibi-di, Jibi-da,* in Folk Dances from Old Homelands, pp. 26-7.

SWEDEN

After decorating the houses with garlands and greens, the young people erect a Maypole and

[1] Folk Songs of Many Peoples, Vol. 1, pp. 143-4.

THE EVE OF ST. JOHN

dance around it by the light of the midnight sun. The merrymaking and dancing continue until dawn.

The bonfires are heaped with fresh fuel. The young people fasten bright flowers to the doorways and erect the Maypole in front of the middle arch opposite the bonfire at the outer point of the triangle. The *Carrousel,* in Folk Dances and Singing Games, pp. 20-1, is vigorously danced about the tree and the festival ends with a lively waltz around and between the St. John's fires.

APPENDIX

ADDITIONAL CUSTOMS FOR SUBSTITUTION IN MIDSUMMER FESTIVAL

ITALY

Flower-crowned children bathe in the river at dawn and return in procession to the village square.

A line of gaily dressed, flower-wreathed boys and girls winds slowly across the stage singing:

> There are three white doves a-flying (3
> By the sea they cry. (3
>
> In the waves they dip their soft wings, (3
> Then soar to the sky. (3[1]

[1] Folk Songs of Many Peoples, Vol. 2, pp. 262-4.

THE EVE OF ST. JOHN

The procession disorganizes in the centre of the stage where the *Tarantella,* in Folk Dances and Singing Games, pp. 86-9, is danced.

RUSSIA

According to an ancient folk belief, the blood red flowers of the fern which blooms but once a year on the Eve of Ivana Kupala (*St. John*) *will bring the heart's desire to those finding it. The search for the mystic blossom is beset with great dangers, and there are few who succeed in the quest.*

The scene shifters place the birch trees irregularly around the stage to simulate a forest. The lighting must be carefully arranged to suggest mystery and horror in the forest and to cast shadows of trees and human figures against the background.

Luba, a village maiden in holiday attire, enters timidly through the left centre door. The music of "Night," in Folk Songs of Many Peoples, Vol. I, pp. 103-4, is softly played as Luba looks fearfully to the right and left and finally grows confused and loses her way. As the girl hesitates, a band of *roussalki* appear from among the trees and dance around her to the accompaniment of "In the Orchard, in the Garden," in Folk Songs of Many Peoples, Vol. I, p. 99. The roussalki circle toward and away from Luba with slow,

THE EVE OF ST. JOHN

gliding movements emphasized by sharp angles in wrists, elbows and knees. They are water nymphs who delight in enchanting forest wayfarers and luring them into the water, and are represented as very pale, slender women with flowing hair and greenish, clinging robes. Luba is frightened but as she looks toward heaven and makes the sign of the cross the roussalki dance away. As Luba at length continues her journey she is suddenly threatened by a group of *vedmi* who stand about in a semicircle uttering wierd shrieks and shaking their broomsticks at her. One of the number comes near Luba and performs the "Russian Dance," in Popular Folk Games and Dances, p. 48. When the dancer stamps, the surrounding vedmi stamp and crowd toward Luba, who shrinks backward. The vedmi are witches with loose hair and long tails who hold rendezvous on the Eve of *Ivana Kupala* and have the power of changing themselves into cats. They are dressed in long white chemises touching the ground. Luba once more makes the sign of the cross and the vedmi disappear in the darkness. Thunder rumbles in the distance; the hooting of owls and barking of dogs are heard but Luba stumbles on. As the music of "Petrus," in Folk Songs of Many Peoples, Vol. 1, pp. 110-11, is being played a *leshij* beckons enticingly from behind a tree. He, too, vanishes however, as Luba makes

THE EVE OF ST. JOHN

the sign of the cross. The leshij is a little, old, bearded man in bark costume who waylays woodland travellers and tickles them to death. Luba, well-nigh exhausted, struggles onward but pauses to listen as the village chimes are heard in the distance striking the hour of midnight. She looks down at the ground, then falls on her knees in rapt relief, for there among the mosses she spies the object of her quest—the red blossom of the fern. As she bends over to look at it, her face is bathed in its glowing radiance. Clasping her hands in joy Luba looks up and sees standing before her her smiling lover who has appeared from behind a tree.

FINLAND

A little before midnight, peasants drive in birch-trimmed carts to the village green where a Maypole, entwined with flowers and leaves, has been erected. They dance about the Maypole and leap over the bonfires surrounding it until long past midnight. Song contests in the open are a part of the night's festivities.

The Maypole is erected and three bonfires built as directed under France and Sweden of the text. All dance around the Maypole *Alands Flicka*, in Folk Dances and Games, pp. 2-3, and the men jump over the fires. The men then group themselves opposite the girls at one side of the stage

THE EVE OF ST. JOHN

and the song contest begins. The men sing the "Gay Young Bachelor," in Folk Songs of Many Peoples, Vol. 1, p. 23, and the girls respond with "The Lovely Rose," *ibid.*, pp. 15-16. The men then follow with "Far in the Forest," *ibid.*, pp. 20-21. The refrain is sung by the girls. All go off the stage while singing.

THE FEAST OF INGATHERING
The Harvest Homing of Many Peoples

THE FEAST OF INGATHERING

PRODUCTION NOTES

STAGE SETTING

The set is semicircular in form and measures forty feet across. A wooden lattice twelve feet high with a five-foot opening in the centre back and two doors, two and one-half by nine feet inserted at regular intervals on either side of the opening forms the background. The doors are made by stretching muslin or canvas over wooden frames and are painted yellow, stippled with green and purple and decorated in Slavic designs with purple, yellow and red. The doors open outward toward the audience and are arranged with fastenings on the inner side. Grape vines with numerous clusters of purple grapes are woven through the lattice background between and over the doors. At a distance of two feet back of the centre opening is a brilliant screen of yellow, red and gold autumn leaves. The space between the stage set and the screen thus acts as a picturesque exit and entrance for groups coming from the right and left. It is flooded with golden light, to produce the illusion of a sunlit path on an autumn

THE FEAST OF INGATHERING

day. A finished sheaf and a pile of ripe grain are placed on the stage at either side of the centre opening.

No curtain is needed between the episodes as the scenery shifts are made by children in Old World costumes.

Costuming and Properties

"National Costumes of the Slavic Peoples," published by The Womans Press, New York, 1920, price $2.00, gives excellent practical suggestions for making Slavic costumes.

The following numbers of the *National Geographic Magazine* will prove extremely helpful in planning costumes for the countries indicated:

Bulgaria—April 1915, Vol. 27, pp. 378-99; Oct. 1915, Vol. 28, p. 390.
Czecho-Slovakia—Dec. 1918, Vol. 34, pp. 491-4; Feb. 1921, Vol. 39, pp. 120-55; Feb. 1923, Vol. 43, pp. 157-60.
France—Nov. 1915, Vol. 28, pp. 392-3, 411-32, 435, 451-4; Nov. 1917, Vol. 32, p. 508; Dec. 1918, Vol. 34, p. 525; July 1921, Vol. 40, pp. 29-44; Feb. 1923, Vol. 43, pp. 149-60.
Greece—Dec. 1922, Vol. 42, pp. 583, 585, 589, 609-29.
Hungary—Dec. 1918, Vol. 34, pp. 485, 495-6, 498-500; Feb. 1923, Vol. 43, pp. 162, 165, 167.
Italy—June 1915, Vol. 27, p. 613; Nov. 1915,

THE FEAST OF INGATHERING

Vol. 28, pp. 446-9; Oct. 1916, Vol. 30, pp. 298-301, 313, 342, 346, 350-9; Feb. 1923, Vol. 43, pp. 181-96.
Poland—Feb. 1923, Vol. 43, p. 161.
Russia—July 1917, Vol. 32, p. 85; Sept. 1917, Vol. 32, p. 239.

Authentic colored prints illustrating the national costumes, folk festivals and customs of many races may be obtained from twenty-five cents upward through Rudolf Lesch, 225 Fifth Avenue, New York City. Scandinavian prints may be purchased from thirty-five cents upward through Albert Bonnier, 561 Third Avenue, New York City.

The grapes, vines and autumn leaves are effectively made from crêpe paper. Free charts and working instructions for the same will be furnished upon written request to the Dennison Manufacturing Company, Service Department, Fifth Avenue and Twenty-sixth Street, New York City.

Folk Songs and Dances

FOLK SONGS OF MANY PEOPLES, with English versions by American poets, by F. H. Botsford. 2 vols. The Womans Press, New York, 1921-2. Price $2.75 and $3.50.

FOLK DANCES AND SINGING GAMES, by Elizabeth Burchenal. Schirmer, New York, 1909. Price $1.50.

FOLK DANCES FROM OLD HOMELANDS, by Elizabeth Burchenal. Schirmer, New York, 1922. Price $1.50.

FOLK DANCES OF FINLAND, by Elizabeth Burchenal. Schirmer, New York, 1915.

FOLK DANCES AND GAMES, by Caroline Crawford. Barnes, New York, 1909. Price $1.50.

POPULAR FOLK GAMES AND DANCES, by M. R. Hofer. Flanagan, Chicago, 1907. Price $.75.

DURATION OF PERFORMANCE

About an hour and a quarter.

PROGRAM

The names of the various nations, with the accompanying italicized description of the customs, should appear on the program, so that the festival theme may be clearly understood by those not already possessing knowledge of European peasant life and customs.

OUTLINE OF FESTIVAL

POLAND (near Krakow)

The last woman reaper is wrapped up in the last sheaf, is called the Baba *or Old Woman, and is taken triumphantly to the farmhouse. There the entire family pour water over her to insure rain for another year.*

Men, women and children are binding the grain into sheaves in rhythm with the music of the harvest folk song they sing:

THE FEAST OF INGATHERING

Down in the meadow the sun is shining
And labor hastens the hours that run—
Happier still, all joys combining,
Now to be with lovely Mary,
With my only one.[1]

The last woman reaper is bound in a sheaf with only her head visible and is set down joyously in the middle of the stage. All dance around her the *Krakoviak,* in Popular Folk Games and Dances, p. 44, or the *Cracoviac,* in Folk Dances from Old Homelands, pp. 48-50. The *Baba* is then gaily carried amid cheers and shouts to the door at the right. The master and mistress greet the harvesters at the doorway and all go through the ceremony of sprinkling her with water.

HUNGARY

The peasants come rejoicing from the fields and join in song and dance.

To the music and words of "Rare the Barley," in Folk Songs of Many Peoples, Vol. 1, pp. 172-3, the men and girls dance *Csárdás* No. 2, in Folk Dances and Singing Games, pp. 61-4. After dancing, the harvesters make a joyous exit through the path at the centre left.

GREECE

The master addresses his vineyard, which gives him good advice.

[1] Folk Songs of Many Peoples, Vol. 1, pp. 77-9.

THE FEAST OF INGATHERING

A Greek husbandman comes to examine the grapes. He plucks bunches here and there, tastes them, makes a wry face, throws them from him and sings:

> Old vineyard mine—go to—
> Cursed vineyard mine!
> A vineyard God-forsaken,
> By the salty sea!

A male chorus behind the scenes sings with the quavering voices of aged men:

> Don't sell me, pray, you fool,
> Good master mine!
> Don't turn me into pennies,
> By the salty sea!

> But hire a young man, do, you fool,
> To dig me deep,
> And an old man to prune me,
> By the salty sea![1]

FINLAND

The villagers assemble at the farm where haymaking or harvesting is going on and work steadily until nightfall. The day ends with singing and a candle-light dance to the strains of the violin.

A double-line procession of reapers, carrying rakes and sickles over their shoulders, enters from right and left down the centre path. They dance

[1] Folk Songs of Many Peoples, Vol. 2, pp. 309-11.

THE FEAST OF INGATHERING

the "Harvest Dance," in Folk Dances and Games, pp. 13-17, or in Folk Dances of Finland, pp. 8-11. "Because of its developed pantomimic expression, it (the Harvester Dance) occupies a very high place among the early types of folk drama. The story of the summer's life is told with the *naïveté* of childhood. The bit of a love story at the end of the dance is an integral part of the whole and forms the climax of the summer's life. The rhythm most prominent in the dance comes from the movement of the reapers."[1]

BULGARIA

The last sheaf of the Bulgarians, known as the Corn Queen, is dressed in women's clothes, carried through the village and finally drowned to insure plenty of rain and dew for the next year's crops.

As the peasants prepare their Corn Queen they sing "Buriano," in Folk Songs of Many Peoples, Vol. 1, p. 185. Raising the Queen aloft, they wind around the stage in gay procession and finally take her down the path at the left centre amid joyous shouts. A great splash is made behind the scenes to denote the drowning.

CZECHO-SLOVAKIA

The end of the harvest is a time of rejoicing

[1] Folk Dances and Games, p. 13.

THE FEAST OF INGATHERING

and thanksgiving in every household. Posviceni, or harvest celebrations, take place in different villages from the middle of August on into the autumn. *The peasant folk present the master of the village with a wreath of grain and field flowers in token of the completed harvest. The festivities end with dancing, singing and feasting.*

A girl crowned with a gay harvest wreath is led to the door at the left centre of the stage and is welcomed by the village landlord and his wife. The landlord is ceremoniously presented with the wreath. The peasants dance the *Rovenacka*, in Folk Dances and Games, pp. 72-3, while a feast table is being brought out and loaded with holiday dishes such as roast pig, goose and special cakes. After feasting and drinking, a girl sings "I'll Have No Other One," in Folk Songs of Many Peoples, Vol. 1, pp. 135-6. Honza, her sweetheart, joins her and together they sing the "Ráda Song," *ibid.*, p. 141.

APPENDIX

Additional Customs for Substitution in Harvest Festival

FRANCE

After gathering grapes from the vines, men and maidens joyfully perform the Vintage Dance.

THE FEAST OF INGATHERING

Grapes are picked from the lattice background by young and old, who then form in procession for the "Vintage Dance," in Folk Dances and Games, pp. 68-70. "The plot of this dance, which is similar to the Harvest Dance of Finland, is composed of the most important incidents of the summer's history. The breaking of the earth in the spring and the gathering of the fruit after the summer's labors are climaxes that force themselves to be represented in the joyful celebration which occurs when the grapes are all harvested. It is danced merrily and madly after the last bunch has been gathered from the vines."[1]

AUSTRIA

In some sections of the country a mock wedding attends the binding of the last sheaf. The woman performing this act is crowned with a wreath of wheat and autumn flowers and is taken, with groom and bridesmaids, to a tavern where everyone dances and makes merry until dawn.

The peasants joyfully crown their wheat bride and lead the bridal party three times around the stage, making an exit by the centre left path.

ITALY

The grapes are gathered amid song and dance, merrymaking and rejoicing.

[1] Folk Dances and Games, p. 68.

THE FEAST OF INGATHERING

The girls and men sing folk songs as they work: "O Fisherman on the Waves," "I'd Like to Die" and "Under the Garden Trees I Picked Finochi," in Folk Songs of Many Peoples, Vol. 2, pp. 264-5, 225 and 268-9. Setting down their baskets laden with grapes, all dance the *Tarantella,* in Folk Dances and Singing Games, pp. 86-9.

FOLLOWING THE STAR
A Festival of Yuletide Songs and Customs

FOLLOWING THE STAR

PRODUCTION NOTES

STAGE SETTINGS

The set is semicircular in form and measures forty feet across. A wooden lattice twelve feet high covered with branches of fir, holly and scarlet berries, forms the background. In the centre of the lattice is inserted a balcony three feet high, three feet long, and one foot wide, with four stairs leading to it from the stage floor at the right and left. Two French windows, each measuring six feet high by eighteen inches wide, open outward from the balcony platform. At the left of the balcony two doors two and one-half by nine feet are inserted into the background at equal distances apart. At the right of the balcony a fireplace, three feet high by four feet wide, and another door are placed in juxtaposition to the doors opposite. The doors open outward toward the audience and are painted a soft-toned red with Slavic decorations of yellow, green and blue. The balcony, stairs and window frames are painted in corresponding fashion. The fireplace is red. The French windows are made from draughtsman's paper painted to simulate panes of glass. When

FOLLOWING THE STAR

opened, the windows disclose a midnight sky and low-hilled horizon. A brilliant (electric) star shines in the sky. A platform three feet high, two feet wide, and five or six feet long, occupies the space behind the stage between the window frame and the sky background. A wooden screen, four by four feet, painted to represent a gray stone wall over which a small vine is climbing, is placed in front of the fireplace to effect the change from indoors to out of doors scenes. Fir trees of various sizes are placed at irregular intervals against the background. A rich piece of foreign tapestry is thrown over the balcony and hangs to the floor.

A curtain is needed between Parts I and II and Parts II and III. No curtain is used between the various episodes of Part II, as the scenery shifts are made in view of the audience by children in Old World costumes.

Costuming and Properties

"National Costumes of the Slavic Peoples," published by The Womans Press, New York, 1920, price $2.00, gives excellent practical suggestions for making Slavic costumes.

The following numbers of the *National Geographic Magazine* will prove extremely helpful in planning costumes for the countries indicated:

Albania—April 1915, Vol. 27, p. 414; Feb. 1923, Vol. 43, pp. 168-9.
Czecho-Slovakia—Dec. 1918, Vol. 34, pp. 491-4; Feb. 1921, Vol. 39, pp. 120-55; Feb. 1923, Vol. 43, pp. 157-60.
France—Nov. 1915, Vol. 28, pp. 392-3, 411-32, 435, 451-4; Nov. 1917, Vol. 32, p. 508; Dec. 1918, Vol. 34, p. 525; July 1921, Vol. 40, pp. 29-44; Feb. 1923, Vol. 43, pp. 149-60.
Greece—Dec. 1922, Vol. 42, pp. 583, 585, 589, 609-29.
Hungary—Dec. 1918, Vol. 34, pp. 485, 495-6, 498-500; Feb. 1923, Vol. 43, pp. 162, 165, 167.
Italy—June 1915, Vol. 27, p. 613; Nov. 1915, Vol. 28, pp. 446-9; Oct. 1916, Vol. 30, pp. 298-301, 313, 342, 346, 350-9; Feb. 1923, Vol. 43, pp. 181-96.
Jugo Slavia—April 1915, Vol. 27, pp. 419, 425-32; Oct. 1915, Vol. 28, p. 389; Dec. 1918, Vol. 34, p. 474; Aug. 1919, Vol. 36, p. v.
Poland—Feb. 1923, Vol. 43, p. 161.
Spain and Spanish America—Dec. 1918, Vol. 34, pp. 519, 521; Feb. 1923, Vol. 43, p. 170; March 1923, Vol. 43, pp. 258-9, i-xvi; April 1923, Vol. 43, p. 1.
Ukraine—Dec. 1918, Vol. 34, pp. 458-61.

Authentic colored prints illustrating the national costumes, folk festivals and customs of many races may be obtained from twenty-five cents upward through Rudolf Lesch, 225 Fifth Avenue, New York City. Scandinavian prints may be purchased from thirty-five cents upward through Albert Bonnier, 561 Third Avenue, New York City.

Many of the properties and costume accessories may be made with the aid of crêpe paper, colored sealing wax, etc. Free charts and working instructions for these things will be furnished upon written request to the Dennison Manufacturing Company, Service Department, Fifth Avenue and Twenty-Sixth Street, New York City.

NATIVITY GROUP

A careful study of nativity paintings by the Old Masters should be made before attempting to costume or group the Holy Family. The flower-like pose of the Virgin in the "Nativity" by Antonio Rosselino at the Metropolitan Museum in New York is particularly suggestive for a folk festival. Prints or postcards of this picture are obtainable through the Metropolitan Museum, Fifth Avenue and Eighty-Second Street, New York City. The Perry Pictures Company, Malden, Massachusetts, has inexpensive reproductions of the world's greatest Holy Family pictures.

The Virgin should be a young woman chosen for purity of type and face. She may be effectively, though not traditionally, costumed in a

FOLLOWING THE STAR

flowing cream-colored robe and long blue veil bound closely over the forehead with a salmon pink band and allowed to hang loosely over the back of the head. By this means the hair is concealed and a somewhat impersonal and therefore universal character is given to the one taking the part of the Virgin. The Virgin kneels on a bed of straw within which a powerful electric light bulb, covered with rose paper, is hidden. The radiance from the light floods the Virgin's face in a manner suggestive of Correggio's "Holy Night."

Folk Songs and Dances

CHRISTMAS AND NEW YEAR SONGS, reprinted from the first and second volumes of Folk Songs of Many Peoples. The Womans Press, New York, 1922. Price $.50.

FOLLOWING THE STAR, by J. P. Scott. Schirmer, New York. Price $.60.

FOLK DANCES AND SINGING GAMES, by Elizabeth Burchenal. Schirmer, New York, 1909. Price $1.50.

Duration of Performance

About one hour and three-quarters.

Programs

It is suggested that the programs be printed in the three sections indicated by Parts I, II, and III. Under Part II the names of the various nations with the accompanying italicized description of

FOLLOWING THE STAR

the custom should appear on the program so that the festival theme may be clearly understood by those not already possessing knowledge of European peasant life and customs.

OUTLINE OF FESTIVAL

PART I

Following the Star

Once, in old Judea's skies,
Shepherds saw a star arise,
Shining through the silent night
With a radiance heavenly bright.
So they followed where it led
To a tiny manger bed,
Where 'mid lowly, humble things
Lay the King of Kings.

Come, ye people, join that train
Winding o'er Judea's plain.
See the nations, near and far,
Following that star.

From the West and from the East
Come we now to keep the feast,
Bearing gifts both rich and rare
For the newborn Savior there.
Sounds of conflict all shall cease,
Hail we now the Prince of Peace.
See the nations from afar
Following that star.

Come, ye people, join that train, etc.

FOLLOWING THE STAR

Echoing down the ages long
Still we hear that old, old song,
Filling all the air again,
"Peace on Earth, good will to men!"
Star of Bethlehem, Star of Light,
Shine into our weary night;
We are pilgrims from afar
Following that star.

Come, ye people, join that train, etc.[1]

As the curtain is drawn, the Holy Family, consisting of Mary, Joseph and the Child, are grouped in tableau form on the straw in the centre-back of the stage. The French windows are open and the star shines brightly in the sky. Fir trees hide the fireplace, balcony steps and doors. A soloist and chorus behind the scenes sing "Following the Star." As the first verse is being sung, four shepherds, bearing their staves and humble field gifts consisting of a large red apple, a sheaf of wheat, a handful of nuts and a bunch of flowers, approach the stage from the back of the auditorium, mount the stage steps at the left, lay their presents before the Christ Child and stand or kneel in silent adoration. At the beginning of the second stanza, three Wise Men, clad in costly raiment and carrying rich gifts of gold, frankincense and myrrh, approach the stage steps at the right, and present their gifts to the Child.

[1] Following the Star, by John Prindle Scott.

A French-Canadian shepherdess enters at the left of the tableau and her companions at the right. In dramatic fashion she replies to the inquiries of her friends and sings of all she has seen at the stable.

Companions: Shepherdess, whence come you (2
              Whence come you?

Shepherdess: From the stable yonder.
              As I walked this night
              I have seen a wonder
              Shining all so bright.[1]

CURTAIN

PART II

THE FESTIVAL IN OTHER LANDS

UKRAINE

SCENE: Out of doors. Balcony windows closed.

On Christmas Eve boys and men carrying an illumined paper star go singing from house to house. In return for their songs they are rewarded with such gifts as chickens, cakes and coins. The custom is termed Kolyada.

A procession of men and boys following their leader, who carries an illumined star, forms behind the scenes and passes singing behind the

---

[1] Christmas and New Year Songs, pp. 27-8.

FOLLOWING THE STAR

balcony windows, entering the stage through the extreme left door. If the light behind the windows is brilliant, the procession will appear in silhouette form to the audience. The boys and men stop before each door singing:

> Yuletide wakes, Yuletide breaks,
> Woman, give me eggs and cakes.[1]

At every door presents are received from master and mistress standing within.

ITALY

SCENE: Indoors. Balcony windows closed. Stage dim except for light of the fire. A low stool stands before the fireplace.

Befana, the gift-bearer of the Italians, is regarded with great awe by the children, whose mothers warn them that the Befana will fetch and eat them if they are naughty. According to legend, the Befana was too busy with her sweeping to accompany the Wise Men in their quest for the Christ Child. For this reason she is often represented as carrying a broom. Every Epiphany she comes down the chimneys and searches in vain for the Infant Christ. The children prepare for the Befana's arrival by carefully emptying the pockets of their garments and hanging them about the hearth. All good children are re-

---

[1] Christmas and New Year Songs, p. 11.

warded by the Befana with confections while those who are bad get only ashes or rods of birch.

Eight boys and girls carrying bright garments come through the balcony windows and down the stairs at the right and left. The scene is full of spirit and childish humor as the garments are shaken out, the pockets emptied and everything arranged for the Befana's coming. Finally, sitting on the floor about the hearth, the children sing drowsily and reverently:

> Slumber, slumber, Lovely Babe,
> Heavenly King; (2
> Slumber, slumber, Little Pet;
> Lullaby, my Little Darling.
> Hear me sing—
> Thou art gracious as a lily.[1]

After singing, the children quietly steal away through the doors at the right and left. The Befana comes down the chimney with her gifts of confections and switches. After she leaves there is a pause; then the stage grows gradually bright and the children rush gleefully down the balcony steps. A merry scramble ensues as the pockets are emptied and the candies eaten. Those receiving switches turn away crying, but are soon beckoned back by the good children, who share their sweetmeats with them. All dance the *Ta-*

[1] *Christmas and New Year Songs*, pp. 41-3.

rantella, in Folk Dances and Singing Games, pp. 86-9.

CZECHO-SLOVAKIA

SCENE: Out of doors.

In certain hillside towns it is customary for young shepherds, carrying a "Bethlehem" or model of the manger scene, to go from house to house singing Christmas hymns and carols.

Roughly clad shepherds singing the "Bohemian Christmas Carol," in Christmas and New Year Songs, p. 12, are greeted at the doors by the peasant folk, who give them gifts of food and drink.

HUNGARY

SCENE: Indoors. Lights dim.

The children believe that an angel from heaven enters the window on Christmas Eve with a tree and a basket of presents. When the angel has finished her work, a bell is rung and the children rush into the room to see their gifts. Later in the evening the entire family join in singing Christmas carols.

The balcony windows open and an angel enters softly, bearing a basket of presents and a small Christmas tree trimmed with a silver star and silver icicles. The angel places the tree on the balcony and busily takes presents from her basket until a bell is heard. She steps back through the window and children and parents burst through the doors to see what has been brought. After examining the presents, all sing the "Christmas Carol," in Christmas and New Year Songs, p. 13, and later dance the Magyar Solo, *Csárdás* No. 2, in Folk Dances and Singing Games, pp. 60-4.

GREECE

SCENE: Out of doors.

On January first, the Day of St. Basil, Athenian street singers go from door to door carrying a model of "St. Basil's Ship," symbolizing the vessel in which the saint made his voyage from Caesarea. Pennies are collected in the boat as the singers chant their New Year's greetings.

> St. Basil comes and passes by,
> And scorns us for no reason why;
> He comes from Caesarea town.
> Mistress, bring us something down.[1]

SPAIN AND SPANISH AMERICA

SCENE: Indoors. Stage dim except for light from fireplace.

According to an ancient and well-loved Spanish folktale, the Holy Kings of the East go each year

[1] Christmas and New Year Songs, pp. 46-7.

FOLLOWING THE STAR

to Bethlehem to pay homage to the Infant Christ and on their journey thither pass through Spain, leaving gifts of sweetmeats and pretty playthings for all good children. Hence, on the Eve of the Epiphany Feast, the children fill their shoes with straw for the Wise Men's horses, place them on the balconies and retire early. In the morning the straw is gone and their shoes are laden with presents.

The children, ready for bed, troop into the room carrying their shoes and hands full of straw. Sitting in a semicircle they stuff their shoes with the straw while singing softly:

Scatter the candies, scatter the sweets now,
For all the children are wanting to eat now.[1]

The children go to the fireplace, light tapers, and, carrying shoes and tapers, mount the balcony steps and place their shoes in a row outside the window. Peering out into the night, they sing:

From the East there came forth three Wise Men,
Seeking Bethlehem town to adore
Jesus Savior, born there in a manger,
Who will reign Son of God evermore.

After singing, the children close the windows, scamper down the stairs and run off to bed. A light outside the windows announces approaching

[1] Christmas and New Year Songs, pp. 24-6.

dawn. The shadowy forms of the Three Kings are silhouetted against the windows as they pass onward toward the East.

CURTAIN

PART III

ADESTE FIDELES

SCENE: Same as Part I.

The curtains are drawn, showing the nativity tableau with the star shining in the sky as at the opening of the festival. Wise men and shepherds are grouped in adoration about the Christ Child. Massed to the right and left of the Holy Family are the representatives of all the nations taking part. After a slight pause, audience and national groups join in singing *Adeste Fideles*.

APPENDIX

ADDITIONAL CUSTOMS FOR SUBSTITUTION IN CHRISTMAS FESTIVAL

PART I

POLAND

May be substituted for French-Canadian group.

SCENE: Nativity Tableau.

Little Polish girls enter timidly at the right and

FOLLOWING THE STAR

left of the stage, look toward Christ Child and softly sing:

> Lullaby, little Pearl,
> Dear baby Jesu,
> Lullaby, little Pearl,
> Dear Baby sleeping;
> Lullaby, little One,
> Dear baby Jesu,
> Mary is holding You,
> Guarding and keeping.[1]

PART II

ALBANIA

SCENE: Indoors.

On New Year's Eve a feast is prepared in every household. Straw is laid under the cloth in memory of the manger birth.

The mother of the family sets the table with food and drink. A large cake made with honey and nuts boasts as many gaily lighted candles as there are members in the household. A gold piece, hidden within the cake, brings good luck for all the year to the one finding it.

SWEDEN

SCENE: Indoors.

A Christmas tree, wired with many colored bulbs, is placed in the centre of the stage.

[1] Christmas and New Year Songs, pp. 6-7.

Old and young dance around the Christmas tree and sing:

'Tis Christmas time, O 'tis Christmas time again!
And after Christmas follows Easter.
No, that is not so, ah no, that is not so,
For Lent, alas! comes in between them.[1]

JUGO SLAVIA (Croatia and Serbia)

SCENE: Indoors.

The day before Christmas the ceremony of the hewing of the Christmas tree for the Badnjak *log takes place. The tree must touch no other branches in its fall and must face toward the East. The Badnjak log is laid in the fireplace at midnight and is burned with great solemnity.*

The housemother lights two tall tapers, sets one on either side of the threshold and, seating herself among the other women who are semi-circularly grouped, watches the *badnjak* log being brought over the sill. As it is lifted into the room the son sprinkles the log with grain. After it is laid in the fireplace the father sings the following song, turns and makes the sign of the cross over each child's head and then embraces each in token of universal love and brotherhood.

[1] Christmas and New Year Songs, p. 40.

Joyous you shall be today; Jesus Christ the Lord
In this holy hour is born, hear the blessed word!
Christ is born, his name praise!
Come to Bethlehem's manger on this day of days![1]

The father casts a silver coin, salt, corn and honey on the log and then goes to the other side of the room, where he lights the incense his grandson holds in a copper dish. This act is to drive away evil spirits from the Christmas Eve supper.

[1] Christmas and New Year Songs, pp. 14-5.

SELECTED BIBLIOGRAPHY OF FESTIVAL MATERIAL

GENERAL

Association of Neighborhood Workers, Arts and Festivals Committee. A Guide and Index to Plays, Festivals and Masques. N. Y., Harper, 1913.

Burchenal, Elizabeth. May Day Celebrations. N. Y., Russell Sage Foundation, Department Child Hygiene, Pub. No. 53, 1910.

Chubb, Percival, and others. Festivals and Plays. N. Y., Harper, 1912.

Commission on Church Pageantry and Drama. The Production of Religious Drama: a Primer. N. Y., Protestant Episcopal Church, Department of Missions, 1922.

Valuable for production suggestions, many of which are applicable to festivals.

Craig, A. A. T. The Dramatic Festival: a Consideration of the Lyrical Method as a Factor in Preparatory Education. N. Y., Putnam, 1912.

Dykema, P. W. Awakening the Festival Spirit in America—an Educational Opportunity. National Educational Association, Proceedings, 1912, pp. 1023-30.

Gronow, A. S. Old Spring Customs in Germany. *Elementary School Teacher,* Vol. 8, April 1908, pp. 413-22.

Harrison, J. E. Ancient Art and Ritual. London, Williams & Norgate, 1915.

Hofer, Amalie. Significance of Recent National Fes-

SELECTED BIBLIOGRAPHY

tivals in Chicago. N. Y., Russell Sage Foundation, Department Child Hygiene, Pub. No. 3, 1908.

Jenny, F. G. The Comic in German Folk Christmas Plays. *Poet Lore,* Vol. 27, Nov. 1916, pp. 680-99.

Jump, H. A. A Festival of the Nations. *The Survey,* Vol. 24, June 4, 1920, pp. 392-6.

Latham, A. J. Making of a Festival. *Teachers College Record,* Vol. 16, May 1915, pp. 248-64.

Lewisohn, Alice. Religious Seasonal Festivals. *Playground,* Vol. 6, Dec. 1912, pp. 324-8.

Mackay, C. D. Festival Production in Parks and Playgrounds. *Playground,* Vol. 15, Sept. 1921, pp. 362-72.

——The Silver Thread and Other Folk Plays. N. Y., Henry Holt & Co., 1910.

——The Festival of Pomona. *Drama,* Vol. 5, Feb. 1915, pp. 161-71.

Needham, M. M. Folk Festivals: Their Growth and How To Give Them. N. Y., B. W. Huebsch, 1912.

Thomason, C. W. Beauty and the Beast (La Belle et la Bête). Philadelphia, Pa., 1921.

——Bluebeard (Barbe Bleue). Philadelphia, Pa., 1921.

——Cinderella (Cendrillon). Philadelphia, Pa., 1921.

——Red Riding Hood (Chaperon Rouge). Philadelphia, Pa., 1920.

——Three Bears (Les Trois Ours). Philadelphia, Pa., 1921.

Folk Plays for Children. From the Old French. To be given in either English or French.

Wallach, R. T. Social Value of the Festival. *Charities,* Vol. 16, June 2, 1906, pp. 314-20.

SELECTED BIBLIOGRAPHY

Music and Dances

Botsford, F. H. Folk Songs of Many Peoples, with English versions by American poets. N. Y., The Womans Press. 2 Vols. 1921-22.

Burchenal, Elizabeth. Folk Dances and Singing Games. N. Y., Schirmer, 1909.

—— Dances of The People. N. Y., Schirmer, 1913.

—— Folk Dances of Finland. N. Y., Schirmer, 1915.

—— Folk Dances of Denmark. N. Y., Schirmer, 1915.

—— Folk Dances from Old Homelands. N. Y., Schirmer, 1922.

—— and Crampton, C. W. Folk Dance Music. N. Y., Schirmer, 1908.

Crampton, C. W. Folk Dance Book. N. Y., Barnes, 1915.

Crawford, Caroline. Folk Dances and Games. N. Y., Barnes, 1909.

Hofer, M. R. Children's Singing Games. Chicago, Flanagan, 1901.

—— Popular Folk Games and Dances. Chicago, Flanagan, 1907.

Costumes, Arts and Crafts

Chotek, Karel. Folk Art. *Art and Archaeology,* Vol. 11, May 1921, pp. 185-98.

Holme, Charles. Peasant Art in Austria and Hungary. N. Y., *The Studio,* 1911.

—— Peasant Art in Italy. N. Y., *The Studio,* 1913.

—— Peasant Art in Russia. N. Y., *The Studio,* 1912.

—— Peasant Art in Sweden, Lapland and Iceland. N. Y., *The Studio,* 1910.

SELECTED BIBLIOGRAPHY

Joyce, T. A., and Thomas, N. W., editors. Women of All Nations: A Record of Their Characteristics, Habits, Manners, Customs and Influence. London, Cassell, 1908-09. 2 Vols.

National Geographic Magazine, Washington, National Geographic Society, 1888 to date.

Pratt, M. S. National Costumes of the Slavic Peoples. N. Y., The Womans Press, 1920.

Folk Customs and Holidays

Calderón de la Barca, F. E. I. Description of *Posadas.* (In "Life in Mexico," Vol. 2, pp. 39-41.) Boston, Little, Brown, 1843. 2 Vols.

Chambers, Robert. Book of Days: a Miscellany of Popular Antiquities in Connection with the Calendar. Edinburgh, W. & R. Chambers, 1873. 2 Vols.

Folk Lore: a Quarterly Review of Myth, Tradition, Institution and Customs. London, Folk Lore Society, 1890 to date.

Frazer, J. G. Golden Bough: a Study in Magic and Religion. 3d ed. N. Y., Macmillan, 1907-15. 12 Vols.

Garnett, L. M. J. Balkan Home Life. London, Methuen, 1917.

Gerard, Dorothea. One Year. Collection of British Authors. Leipzig, Bernhard Tauchnitz. Vol. 3402.

Polish life and customs.

Greenough, W. P. Canadian Folk-Life and Folk Lore. N. Y., Richmond, 1897.

Hawthorne, Hildegarde. Shepherd Actors of Roumania. *St. Nicholas,* Vol. 39, Dec. 1911, pp. 176-7.

SELECTED BIBLIOGRAPHY

Hazlitt, C. W. Faiths and Folklore: a Dictionary of National Beliefs, Superstitions and Popular Customs. (Great Britain). London, Reeves & Turner, 1905. 2 Vols.

Hearn, Lafcadio. The Romance of the Milky Way. *Atlantic Monthly,* Vol. 96, Aug. 1905, pp. 238-50. Festival of the Weaving Lady of the Milky Way.

Horne, R. H. Great Fairs and Markets of Europe. *Harper's Monthly,* Vol. 46, Feb. 1873, pp. 376-85.

Miles, C. A. Christmas in Ritual and Tradition, Christian and Pagan. London, Unwin, 1912.

Ralston, W. R. S. Songs of the Russian People as Illustrative of Slavonic Mythology and Russian Social Life. London, Ellis & Green, 1872.

Rappoport, A. S. Home Life in Russia. N. Y., Macmillan, 1913.

Revue des Traditions Populaires: Recueil Mensuel de Mythologie, Litterature Orale, Etmographie Traditionelle et Art Populaire. 2 Rue de Lille, Paris, 1886 to date.

Riis, J. A. Yule-tide in The Old Town. *Century,* Vol. 77, Dec. 1908, pp. 163-71.

Rodd, Remell. Customs and Lore of Modern Greece. London, Stott, 1892.

Spicer, D. G. Notes on Syrian Holidays, Customs, Traditions and Superstitions. *Foreign Born,* Vol. 1, Dec. 1919, pp. 1-4.

——Calendar of Foreign Holidays, Festivals and Saints Days. *Ibid.,* Vols. 1-3, Jan. 1920-Aug. 1922.

——Old World Easter Customs. *Ibid.,* Vol. 1, April 1920, pp. 1-4.

——Foreign and Native Carnival Customs. *Ibid.,* Vol. 2, Feb. 1921, p. 129.

SELECTED BIBLIOGRAPHY

——Hîna-no-Sekku, the Feast of Dolls; Folk Customs and Superstitions of Holy Week. *Ibid.,* Vol. 2, March 1921, pp. 135, 136-7.
——Tsing Ming, the Chinese Festival of the Dead; the Festival of St. George. *Ibid.,* Vol. 2, April 1921, pp. 167, 168.
——Old World Building Customs and House Superstitions. *Ibid.,* Vol. 2, May 1921, pp. 199-201.
——Agricultural Folk Customs and Superstitions of the Soil. *Ibid.,* Vol. 2, June 1921, pp. 236-7.
——Port Customs and the Folk Lore of the Harbor. *Ibid.,* Vol. 2, Aug. 1921, pp. 267-9.
——Gift Bearers of Christmas Tide. *Ibid.,* Vol. 2, Dec. 1921, pp. 365-6.
——Old World Schools and Schoolmasters. *Ibid.,* Vol. 3, Feb. 1922, pp. 36-8.
——Folk Festivals of Early Spring. *Ibid.,* Vol. 3, April 1922, pp. 109-10.
——Wanderers and Wayfarers. *Ibid.,* Vol. 3, May 1922, pp. 134-5.
——Legendary Race Origins and Race Founders. *Ibid.,* Vol. 3, June 1922, pp. 172-3.

Stratilesco, Tereza. From Carpathian to Pindus: Pictures of Roumanian Country Life. Boston, Luce, 1907.

Urlin, E. L. Festivals, Holy Days and Saints' Days. London, Simpkin, 1915.

Walsh, W. S. Curiosities of Popular Customs. Philadelphia, Lippincott, 1914.

152